PROJECT MANAGEMENT
for the
NEWER NORMAL

UNLOCK OPPORTUNITIES

JOHN ROBERT

WITH MIKE TEILER

Project Management for the Newer Normal

© 2021 John Robert. All rights reserved.

No part of this publication may be reproduced, distributed, or transmitted in any form or by any means, including photocopying, recording, or other electronic or mechanical methods, without the prior written permission of the author, except in the case of brief quotations embodied in critical reviews and certain other noncommercial uses permitted by copyright law. For permissions visit www.newernormal.com and contact: johnrobert99@gmail.com

First Edition

Dedicated to the project managers and businesses

who strived to get vaccines and medicines

delivered for combating the pandemic

Project Management for the Newer Normal

Table of contents

Foreword
Preface
Introduction   01

Part I: The Pandemic Paradox
1. Normal – New Normal   17
2. The Shift   37.
3. The Missing Process   67

Part II: The Methodology
4. Deconstructing a Large Project   81
5. Need for Mini-projects   87
6. Industrial Revolution and Projects   99
7. The "Art side" of Projects   107

Part III: The Relay Race and Projects
8. Mini-projects and Relay Race   131
9. The Relay Race Metaphor   139
10. How to Create Mini-Projects from A Larger Ones   149

Part IV: Turbocharge Execution
11. Executing Mini-Projects   169

Part V: What's in it for Me?
12. Benefits   187
13. Underlying Principles   197

14. Bonus: Hack the Happy Hormones   205

Extro   215
Bibliography   219
List of illustration   221
Acknowledgments   223
About Authors   225

Foreword

There are many years of project management insight underpinned by common sense and real-world experience well-crafted into this book. It is truly a unique contribution compared to the information that is regurgitated in so many other project management books. John Robert creates a compelling case for changing our traditional approach in how we approach projects in the *new normal*, but more importantly, he goes a step further and shows us how. This book outlines a clear simple framework on how projects can be delivered faster and with more successful outcomes in complex times.

Project management is an Achilles heel for many of the most successful organisations on the planet. The bad news is they are often the very creator of the problems they are trying to solve. The good news is a solution may be hiding in plain sight, but they haven't noticed.

For too long project management has been approached and institutionalised within existing ways of thinking, obsessed with schedule and cost-control. Organisations embrace frameworks and methodologies as a silver bullet or one-size fits all approach to project success but unfortunately, they rarely deliver.

A new revolutionary paradigm shift in how we approach projects is required. This book offers practical but profound insight into the building blocks required to move from talk to walk. For too long project success and strategic project management have been approached on a project, programme and portfolio basis, an obsession with looking up rather than looking down into the project.

This book presents an opportunity to create order out of chaos and approach the complexities of a post-pandemic era with a more focused relay race approach. Success lies in specialist focusing on micro-projects within the project lifecycle rather than generalists focusing on the entire project. However, it is not enough to simply change our project management approach. We need to change our entire way of thinking about projects. Each project is a truly unique challenge requiring an innovative approach. Success lies in brainstorming, innovation, and creativity more so than in the roll-out of tried and tested tools, techniques, and templates that may have worked in the past.

Organisations and society are in a constant state of change and uncertainty, and this requires us to radically rethink the way we approach projects. Part of the answer can be found in recognising project management is both an art and a science and people are the most significant cog in the wheel.

This book is needed now more than ever as more organisations become more projectized in their approach to meet an era of profound change. John Robert brings together the "best of the best" when it comes to best practice project performance and purpose. He offers us an insight into the immense power of people with a purpose in a focused project team. It is a treasure chest full of great ideas, practical advise and lessons learned from project success and failure.

Foreword

The pages that follow offer a compass that points to a new north star, a new approach for a new project world. The traditional "projects as usual" rules of engagement are no longer fit for purpose. It is a thoughtful and stimulating contribution to project management and counter-balances so many other books that focus on processes and tools. Projects have transformed from brick and mortar to complexity and change with a new emphasis on rapid execution cycles and a greater emphasis on learning and reflection.

Thankfully this book is light on theory and more focused on the practical application of what it takes to deliver superior project outcomes. It manages to strip away the theory and cut to the chase of what really works in a complex post-pandemic environment: empowered engaged people.

John McGrath
Project Management Professor
Director of Project Management Programmes at Technological University Dublin
Oct 2021

Project Management for the Newer Normal

Preface

Pandemic has once changed our lives forever, it impacted how we live. Project management is no exception. I would say among others project management is the profession that has got a maximum impact on the pandemic.

Canceled projects, disrupted supply chain, absence of resources, the unpredictability of the future of the projects hover around the life of a project manager. At the same time, we have several super critical and urgent projects that need to be finished at the earliest as well triggered by businesses. This ended up in a paradoxical situation. But one thing is certain, there has been an ongoing and challenging to shorten project lifecycle. This has been intensified because of the pandemic.

In the *new normal*, project teams are facing unprecedented challenges and escalating demands to bring more products to market and to get them there faster than ever before. At the same time, we are witness to forces that tend to complicate the execution of projects and cause them to take longer than before. These forces include the ever-increasing complexity of projects, digitalization, new norms of working, other external elements, and the influence of globalization on the scale and complexity of operations.

While project management ecosystems are shifting gears to enhance cross-functional collaboration, harness the benefits of domain expertise, and leverage learning from experience, businesses need a more holistic approach to accelerate the completion of projects. Be it an idea, innovation or a new product; there is only a specific window of opportunity to gain market acceptance before stellar progress becomes yesterday's stagnation. Project teams have a very limited time to develop a concept, give it shape and deliver a new product or service to market. The need is for leaders to establish winning methodologies to accelerate projects to implement their strategy and achieve their vision, and this demand is ever increasing.

Today, the ability to quickly identify and to adapt to a continually changing undercurrent, short-cycle technology obsolescence, and the global matrix ecosystem is what differentiates winning businesses from all the rest. A successful company needs a simple yet powerful way in which its projects can be executed so that success can be achieved every time. There are multiple project management frameworks attempting this, including mine, which purports to deliver the goods, yet end up becoming just another complex system to handle, requiring considerable training, resources, organizational change, and transformation to reap the benefits. This is because of applying old normal principles in the new ecosystem. Moreover, we ended up with too much jargon, personas, governance, and review mechanisms that need to be implemented in these frameworks.

The following is my humble effort to simplify things by employing the metaphor of the relay race while at the same time providing an empowering framework to unleash the potential of the expert resources employed to execute projects. Thanks to COVID-19, our projects are already complicated enough. The secret to success is to provide a project management framework that serves to simplify rather than to add levels of complexity on top of projects which are already complex by their nature.

The concepts in this book have evolved through reflecting on the swift responses and hands-on practical experience in combating with pandemic; hence do not be surprised to find that it closely resembles real-life situations and addresses practical issues confronted by many project professionals at these times. Mini-project methodology, when complemented by the relay race metaphor, can be an excellent starting point to implement a practical workflow to enhance the velocity of projects while also putting people first. This approach can be implemented if one currently practices an entry-level 'plain vanilla' approach to project management and wants to advance to the next level. Furthermore, a team can easily adapt this methodology to simplify practices without loss of productivity. I have attempted to ensure that this approach can be implemented "on the go" without significant transformational needs allowing a project to reap substantial benefits right from day one. Frankly, no one can afford to wait to harness these benefits.

The mini-project can be designed and implemented in such a way that it empowers people while making them more accountable, increases the speed of execution, fosters uncomplicated communication, enables course correction as an ongoing process, improves respect for individual contribution, enables learning, and facilitates enhanced focus. Try this for your next project; you will find that it can be adopted early and the project can be completed much faster which is critical because you have less and less time to introduce your next product or application or service to the market space.

Can we deliver projects faster than we have ever imagined in the pandemic? The answer always lies with the people involved. This book aims to provide the key to unlocking high performance through people while implementing an exciting and empowering process in the *new normal*.

May success be with you!

John Robert
Oct 2021

Preface

Introduction

The pandemic crisis has introduced an era of frenzied activity that has fundamentally impacted the mindset of many businesses and business leaders. Mainstream, cable and social media, qualify every change as hysteria. 'Experts' scrutinize every decision made by health or governmental decision and criticize them without a hint of the requisite complexity and nuance that such analysis deserves. In response, businesses and leaders have become highly reactive to every change occurring on an almost daily basis. The instability which stems from uncertainty and rapid change often causes leaders to make reflexive decisions that often do more harm than good to the business. It is important to seize the day, but it is no less important to make proactive, well thought out and logical business decisions for the ongoing well-being of the business.

The current crisis is novel to be sure, but this is not the first crisis to be faced, and unfortunately, not the last. A crisis accentuates the need to bring the right products and services to market in the best possible time. A crisis forces us to abandon bad habits that we have allowed ourselves to think that we needed them to remain flexible and robust. The *new normal* is not as much about pushing the accelerator to the floor as it is about adopting those best working practices which result in making the right decisions and executing projects in a smart, risk-managed and responsible way.

In this volume we focus on the best habits and practices that have served us well for years, not only in times of crisis. The lasting beneficial effects of the *new normal* will be in learning to keep what works and abandon or change those practices that have wasted time, resources, and most important, distracted us from reaching the core objectives to drive profitable growth in good times as well as bad.

Delivering projects quickly has become the mainstay in combating the global coronavirus pandemic, whether launching new vaccines, releasing novel therapies for COVID-19 treatment, repurposing of existing medicines to aid in patient recovery, or simply adapting to the new reality of our lives at home, at work, and at school. In parallel, and maybe partially in response, there is a huge surge in digitalization projects and automation. The authors are fortunate to be a part of the healthcare ecosystem and to be involved in this evolution. How projects are conceived, planned, executed, controlled, and closed out has offered newer ways of managing them in the *new normal*. These methods are not commonly taught in traditional project management academia but are based on experiential learning. The remainder of this book is about exploring common-sense methods of simplifying the ever-growing complexity in our project environment.

Part I:

The Pandemic Paradox

The Pandemic Paradox

The pace of change we are all experiencing in the post-COVID-19 pandemic era is unprecedented and the acceleration continues. The challenges that we are facing and the need to deliver on projects quickly are more acute than ever and this affects every industry and every discipline, but project management most of all. As project managers, we embrace this type of challenge and continually evolve. As the saying goes, "when the going gets tough, the tough get going!"

The environment generated by the COVID-19 pandemic has resulted in a paradoxical situation. Many organizations have "lost their balance" and rather than following their long-term strategy, have become hyper-reactive to the situation, at best only partially justified in doing so. On the one hand, many future-facing projects have been canceled in order to free up resources to feed the immediate need of the global supply chain. On the other hand, and this is where it may be less rational, to support the surge in urgent projects that are the need of the hour.

The move to projects to serve the needs arising out of this, or any other crisis is intuitive and understandable, if not always well thought through and rational. The selection of which projects to pursue aggressively must be well considered. Not every company is going to have the technology to cure the virus, though it sometimes appears that every company thinks that they do. The instinct to 'save the world' is strong from both humanistic and commercial perspectives. The question is to what extent this is true, and what the alternative cost is for ongoing projects and initiatives. The vast majority of the projects we were pursuing pre-pandemic remain relevant during and post-pandemic. Curing cancer or Alzheimer's Disease may still be a top priority. By chasing the dreams of the moment we need to understand that, by definition, we are distracted from solving other problems that may be far more impactful in the longer term.

This problem is magnified by a crisis but is not unique to a crisis, and recognizing the implications is key to the *new normal*. All project managers have experienced the tendency by an organization to add new projects to the pipeline. When resources, especially bottleneck resources are under-used it may make good business sense to add new projects, to support future profitable growth. But, what happens when adding projects to a system that is already stressed? Just like adding just a few more cars to a motorway can cause a traffic jam, adding projects in excess to the bottleneck resources will cause a logjam and have the opposite effect upon the organization. Having a realistic estimation of the true throughput of the organization is key to a smoothly running organization, and only a well-streamlined concern can finish projects quickly.

With this in mind, the process of adding new projects must account for capacity and throughput. We want to have a reserve of new projects ready to start, but only when existing projects finish. The solution to low throughput by initiating new projects only works when the system is below capacity. To push more new project starts on a balanced overloaded system will only slow things down. To achieve speed and throughput, focus on finishing the existing projects first, making room for the next projects to progress. Finally, if a new project to address a crisis that is essential, consider in the most rational way which other, ongoing projects should be canceled or deferred to a future date, recognizing that when we stop a project in the middle, we lose the value of what we have already achieved. Is the new project really worth it? If so, make the exchange, but make the decision using cold rationality and logic, not just as a knee-jerk reaction to an emotionally charged situation.

Stop starting, start finishing

We have been witness to disruptions in the supply chain at every level. Original equipment manufacturers (OEMs), raw material suppliers, and contractors have taken a hit. Energy costs have sky-rocketed as availability becomes scarce and the same has occurred with transportation costs by road, rail, sea, and air. We've experienced delays in regulatory inspections and issuing of permits, as agencies have been forced into virtual or paper inspections enabling systems to somehow maintain continuity of function, amid travel restrictions, lockdowns, social distancing and general chaos. Policymakers are reluctant or unable to provide clarity to the world amidst high levels of uncertainty.

On the other hand, we have seen a surge in digitalization to ensure business continuity via work from home, and remote medical treatments, just to note two examples. Traditional physicians' office visits by medical representatives and business conferences and exhibitions have been disrupted forcing us to find innovative ways to interact, all the while longing to get back to human contact and creative collaboration.

On one side there is ever-increasing encouragement to do "more with less". Pressure to maintain profitability and increased focus on reducing expenses continue to increase. CapEx cycles and long burn projects and strategies have been put on the back burner, and instead, projects with quick wins are prioritized. Many new clinical trials were conducted. Suddenly, we have become more open to alternative therapy options. Adaptation to changes in the medical system expanded within the lay community at large as well as elective and non-essential treatments became harder to come by.

On the personal front, individuals and organizations have had to sacrifice jobs, adopt distance learning, reduce bonuses and incentives, and shut down individual enterprises, services, and even entire industries for a period. No words can explain the human suffering the pandemic has inflicted on all of us.

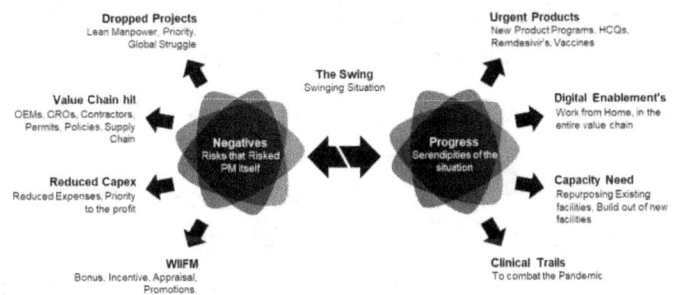

Figure 1: The Pandemic Paradox

Like a phoenix, the world rose from the ashes of this disaster. In projects as well, project teams, contractors, consultants, business owners, and service providers adapted to the *new normal* and found creative and innovative ways to meet the challenges posed, and in many cases to excel beyond levels of past performance. We all learned immensely valuable lessons. In the discipline of project management, we had to adapt to a different ecosystem of managing projects. Many of the changes, those that are truly beneficial and suited to human nature, not simply making the best of a bad situation, will remain, making us stronger, better and more successful. These new and positive adaptations will not only survive the Pandemic but have provided us with an all-new perspective. Call it a silver lining, though hard to call it a blessing, out of adversity and necessity have come invention. These new approaches will continue to be relevant in the emerging economy. Ironically, many of these new adaptations are really not so new to us, but like the creation of a diamond from coal, the result of the surmounting pressure forcing us back to an ideal crystalline form, those best practices, that in better times are convenient to ignore. We can no longer afford to ignore them and we do so at our peril.

There are several projects that we have closely experienced or observed that illustrate these points. Some examples of those that have been executed unconventionally amid the pandemic and the waves of post-pandemic impact, follow:

- Newer software implementations, digital enablements facilitating new ways of working.
- Several companies launched vaccines within six to nine months!

- Remdesivir active pharmaceutical ingredient (API) generic version developed within 48 days.
- Pharma company ramping up the productivity of an age-old medicine called Hydroxychloroquine, multifold in one month
- Several new vaccine manufacturing facilities emerged, seemingly out of nowhere, across the globe and in a record time
- Automation at an unprecedented rate
- Unprecedented focus on Artificial Intelligence initiatives
- 'Travel replacement therapy' for corporate executives
- Massive hospitals were constructed in record time, many of them in 30 days and 45 days. We are not referring to temporary health centers. These hospitals are well constructed to endure in the long term.

We have been personally involved in such initiatives and, to gain additional insights on these projects, we have connected with business leaders who have successfully driven other programs. We were curious to ask them what project management practices they have used to deliver the products to the market at an unprecedented rate. Surprisingly, almost all of them answered something like this;

"We had little time for proper planning, we know what is needed, and management is fully committed to providing resources and funds to deliver these. Hence we started execution directly."

"We did not have time to think about what project management methodology could work for us, all that we need is to deliver the projects faster"

"We were offered a blank check by our CEO. He wanted to start the project yesterday and deliver the product today. He is ok to improve the shortcoming of the first version tomorrow"

Now after reading these comments, one may think that it is counterintuitive, even counterproductive, to begin a project management book with such references. It is a shocking reality that people did not believe that they had time to pause to make a schedule for these super-critical projects. They did not have the patience, discipline, or confidence in project management to spend the few days necessary to elaborate a formal project plan and evaluate which series of activities could help them to deliver these projects faster. In essence, we heard from project execution teams that despite ignoring all project management principles, they successfully executed projects in record time.

So, let's take a closer look at what they actually told us, and the conditions that brought about the stunning successes in project after project.

Keeping your eye on the prize

The pandemic situation gave a whole new meaning to the concept of priority. The needs of the moment were very tangible to every single member of the team and brought crystal clear focus to the project objective. Everyone understood that completion in the shortest possible time was literally a matter of life or death, and maybe even for themselves or their own immediate families. Every single day of progress in bringing the new product, or process, or service to market meant several thousand lives saved even if that day belongs to the preparation of schedule. A well-planned work is half done?

May be;

We believe that there are three important take-away messages for project managers as well as for project methodology and, if we can successfully internalize these messages, an opportunity for gaining even greater speed than was observed in these projects.

First, when we focus on the immediate project at hand that absolutely must be executed "right now!" we have no hesitancy to cancel, or at least ignore all other projects. Suddenly, rather than being "distracted" by a myriad of projects all going on in parallel, we are able to truly prioritize one project above all and put all of our focus on it. This results in a laser focus on a single objective, one task at a time. Focus, finish, and move on! There are no other activities to confuse or distract us and we cannot be sidetracked by other "priorities."

The take-away for the *new normal* is we need to decrease the number of active projects running in parallel, focusing on what is truly critical to be done today. Another way of looking at this is to "stop starting (new projects) and start finishing (ongoing projects.)

Second, we must face a hard reality and ask ourselves if we, as project management professionals tasked with leading our projects, sufficiently motivating our teams? Is it realistic to believe that once the "life or death" nature of the pandemic is behind us that we will be able to arouse the same level of passion? This is our challenge. While take-away number one (eliminate distractions) will be very helpful, we need to focus on our team members. Not that every project is life or death, no, of course not. But that we are all committed to exactly the same priorities with a single-minded focus, and that we are all pulling in one direction.

Finally – we need to be honest with ourselves. If the project team, as experienced as they may be, does not see the benefit that our methodologies are bringing to them, enabling and facilitating the safer, cheaper, and faster completion of projects, then maybe our methodologies are not bringing the value that we thought. This is a scathing indictment of the current "standard" methodologies and we had better do some soul searching.

Project budget

One of the authors is old enough to have very clear memories of July 20th, 1969, the day Apollo 11 landed on the moon, and astronaut Neil Armstrong took that small step for man but made a giant leap for mankind. The mission of Apollo 11 culminated on that day, and, of course, a few days later when the astronauts all returned home safely. However, that historic day was many years in the making. US President John F. Kennedy declared on May 25th, 1961 that an American would land safely on the moon within that decade.

As project managers, we are taught about the triple constraint of budget, scope, and timeline, and we love to joke that you can have any two of these, but not all three.

In the Apollo project, effectively, only two of the three constraints were put in place. 1. Timeline – "within this decade." 2. Scope "returning them safely to Earth." When resources are unlimited, the sky (and the moon!) truly is the limit. In the examples quoted above, like in Apollo, our project teams were offered "a blank check", or "management is fully committed to providing resources." In other words – when we are presented with "unlimited resources" (in reality there is no such thing as truly unlimited resources, but you get the point...) scope and timeline become a lot less challenging to meet.

First, get to market!

'First, get to market' is not the same as 'get to market first.' Both are important guiding principles.

It is a well-accepted maxim that being "first to market" is key to commercial success for the organization, and what is the role of the project manager if not to bring maximum value to the organization? We, the authors, have long believed in the principle of "first, get to market!" But, what does this mean?

Being early to market has a huge impact on market share both in the short term, as well as in the long term. Even more important, reaching a market with less competition means that we can command a better price in the market. The mathematical product of these two factors, greater market share and higher price in the market is a huge commercial and financial advantage for the company, ensuring profitable growth. Understanding this concept helps us focus on the true scope of the project. Makers of high-tech gadgets have long known that it is more important to be first to market than to be the best in the market. This can take many forms.

Features – the first to market the cellular phone, personal digital assistant, or digital music player gained long-term value in their product market segments. Number two-faced an uphill battle, even when offering more and better features. While maintaining market dominance is always a challenge, it is much easier to maintain market position than to try to capture it back from someone else!

Cost of goods – reaching the market first, even with a suboptimal process or expensive materials may appear to be inefficient. Still, from a perspective of price and market share, the long-term benefits of being first to market, far outweigh the temporary inefficiencies of process and costs. First, get to market! From a superior market position, you have time to optimize your process or substitute less expensive materials. First, get to market!

The examples above, of the criticality of time in bringing a new product, process, or service to market really help to focus the mind on the relative importance of the classic "triple constraint" of Time-Cost-Scope. While it is true that resources (budget) are always constrained, and in some ways dictate our capacity (the number of new projects we can deliver over a period of time) – if we do find ourselves in a position where we have to decide between the three; the timing has to be first and budget has to be last. This is a key takeaway reinforced by the circumstances of the *new normal*!

These take-away messages and the ability to have ultimate shared clarity of priority (focus), minimum requirements to reach the market (quality/scope) and high motivation must be implemented in our projects as we move forward under the *new normal* and will facilitate faster project completion, which, in turn, will result in greater project throughput!

The conclusion that "there is no time" to spend the hours, or at most the few days, to create a clear project roadmap is erroneous, and we can guarantee that creating and executing a robust project plan, with clarity of critical (bottleneck!) activities complemented by the *new normal* take-aways will bring more speed to projects than ever before.

In this *new normal*, the only methodology which works is that which brings the product a day earlier to the market. Speed is the key. There is "no time for planning." There are fewer budget constraints. There is no rigid scope definition in the traditional sense.

Having experienced this, we understand that we need to set a new paradigm for how projects are addressed.

So, how should we approach projects? Think again, this is the *new normal*.

Let's start by getting back to basics.

Normal – *New Normal*

It is quite normal to define the boundary conditions of normal, *new normal*, and newer normal before we proceed further.

"*Normal*" is the good old ways we operated and managed projects prior to Feb 2020, the onset of COVID-19 restrictions. "*New Normal*" is from then to yesterday, with the new ways of working we have experienced and witnessed. The *normal* ways of working may not be relevant for today. Let's try to understand why.

COVID-19, left unchecked, naturally mutates into new variants, especially in a global pandemic in which there are as many ways of addressing the pandemic as there are countries trying to combat it. Lockdowns, complete lockdowns, lockdowns with and without restrictions, wearing masks, social distancing, vaccines of different types all have their impact on the numbers and groups of people infected. The more people who are infected, the more the virus replicates and the more opportunity the virus has to mutate and create new variants. These variants may be more or less virulent than the old and may be more or less contagious than the old. As more contagious variants appear, the levels of immunity that protected us in the past are no longer sufficient to protect us going forward, and the cycle of infection continues, occasionally spinning out of control for a time until the health authorities, systems, and governments can respond. Thus, the *new normal* does not remain new for very long and soon we find ourselves facing what we call the *"newer normal."* *Newer normal* refers to the reality that we are going to face from today onwards. As the challenges increase, we will soon see that our resilience and adaptability also increase. Throughout this book, we will be using the terms *new normal* and *newer normal* interchangeably, referring to the future of the project ecosystem. This is all about the future of projects.

Just to re-baseline the traditional processes, there used to be five stages in a project, namely, 1) Initiation, 2) Planning, 3) Executing, 4) Monitoring and Control, and 5) Closing. *If you are an experienced project manager, jump to the next chapter, you must be knowing this well enough.*

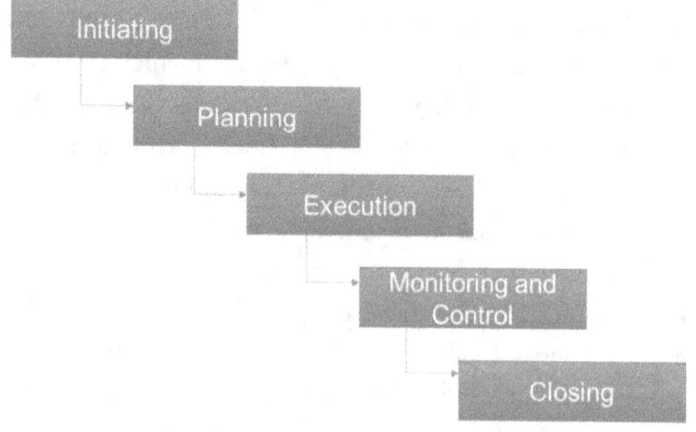

Figure 2: Process Groups in a Project

Be it a megastructure like the Burg Khalifa, Apollo moon mission, Statue of Unity, a new model car, software, next version of iPhone, the house you stay in, a new app, or a new product - all of these are created following the same project management processes.

So let us look at these steps in brief

Step 1: Initiation

Develop a project charter that consists of what needs to be done by who and a budget. This step will mainly define the scope of the project.

Step 2: Planning

Break down the project into several smaller, more manageable steps called tasks. All tasks are arranged in a sequence in order to deliver the product. Tasks may be executed in series or in parallel, this is called the project schedule. Executing all of these tasks successfully and in the right order will result in achieving the goal of the project.

Step 3: Execution

Here is where the rubber meets the road. The actual execution of the tasks as per the schedule prepared in Step 2- Planning.

Step 4: Monitoring and Control

This is the process of regulating time and cost, handling deviations, and managing scope creeps. The objective here is to execute the project as per the pre-determined time, cost, and scope in accordance with the schedule.

Step 5: Closing

Congratulations, you have successfully completed a normal project. Now the product or service derived from the project can be handed over to the next stage for commercialization or implementation. Once the execution is achieved and the project is completed, the product is delivered to the intended customer. During Closing, reconciliation of the cost, time, and lessons learned are reviewed and logged so that the next projects can be done better.

The effort needed across the lifecycle of a project varies. Efforts and resources gradually increase following project initiation until they peak at the height of execution and again reduce towards the end of the project and close out. Efforts are the sum total of the resources (human, equipment, and financial) and time required to execute the activities needed to successfully complete the project.

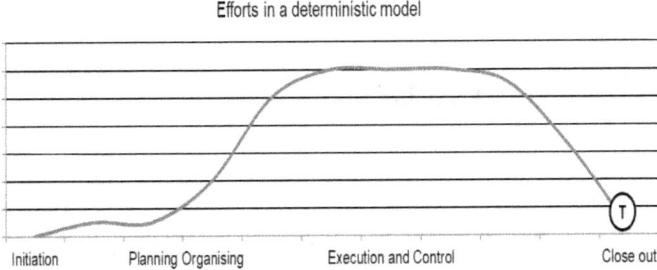

Figure 3: Efforts needed across the project lifecycle

In subsequent chapters, we will learn in detail how to get these processes upgraded for the *new normal*.

Triple Constraints

> *The traditional measures of scope, time, and cost are essential but no longer sufficient in today's competitive environment. The ability of projects to deliver what they set out to do—the expected business benefits—is what organizations need. (PMI, 2018)*

Executing a project can be compared to playing one of my favorite board games from my childhood - "Snakes and Ladders." Using this metaphor is an interesting way to gain an understanding of the journey of a project throughout its lifecycle. In India this game is known as the Paramapadham, meaning attaining the ultimate destination. Every project has a destination to reach and the journey has ups and downs – a perfect metaphor for projects.

In a project, the dice start rolling with the kick-off meeting when a new project gets approved. Then the project progresses through various squares of its lifecycle according to the speed of execution of the respective player. In this journey, some opportunities, just like ladders, can be realized, and some adversities, like the proverbial snakes will, no doubt, be encountered as well! Rolling the dice makes the project advance in a linear fashion. Landing on a ladder makes the project advance exponentially. When a risk manifests, it is like landing on a snake, that delays the project and often even represents a significant setback in the worst case. This is similar to repeated iterations and reworks in a project.

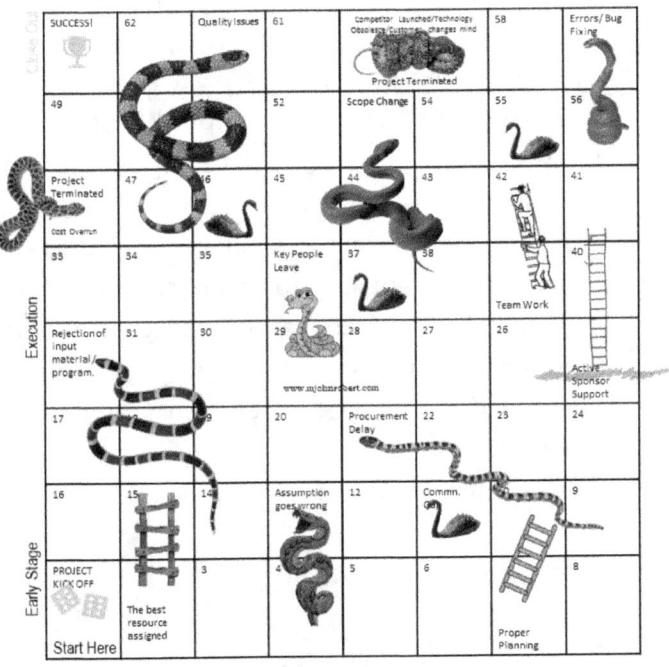

Figure 4: Snake and Ladder game metaphor in projects

A project is filled with both risks and opportunities. Particularly in the *new normal* projects appear to have been 'blessed' with an entire den of the snakes! Let's try to make this metaphor a bit more concrete by bringing some real-world examples of what may represent snakes and ladders in projects. Starting with ladders:

    a. Active sponsor support, particularly in the pandemic, the involvement of sponsors, and

leadership to get the products released in the market – a big positive to projects.
b. The best resources assigned to the project makes the project progress at unprecedented speed
c. Team work, people sharing the vision of the project and aligned towards the objective of the project
d. Gaining top priority for a project, meaning that performing the critical tasks for the project is always the most important task to be performed by the team!
e. 'Blank check' funding, a scenario we witnessed during the pandemic to produce emergency products like vaccines, software to enable work from home, remote schooling or remote physician visits, Artificial Intelligence enabled products, no cost constraint
f. A compelling need for the product, services, or results in the market
g. A compelling business case

Some examples of snakes in projects include:
a) Assumptions made at the beginning of the project were wrong, particularly in the pandemic, where there is a restriction of movement of materials and people from country to country.
b) Communication gaps created by increased work from home/virtual teams that result in chaos in the project
c) Delays in the procurement and delivery of input materials, equipment, or components needed for the project to be carried out successfully, canceled

Triple Constraints

flights and shipments, import restrictions from specific high-risk regions
d) Shortage of input materials, premium pricing, and huge demand outstripping supply
e) Rejection of input material or program that is needed for the project
f) Key people are being sidelined due to illness or quarantine.
g) Change in project scope as a result of a volatile market scenario, customer preference, new policy decisions, funding issues, and technological obsolescence
h) The project becomes unviable due to delays or cost overrun
i) Quality issues, errors, and bugs that adversely impact the product or services
j) Financial fragility, cash reserve challenges, and working capital requirements
k) Fluctuation of commodity prices, and currency exchange rates

All these have an impact on the three legs of the triple constraint.

Time:

Traditionally, project management advocates a target date for project completion, and the entire team works towards that date. All activities are organized in a logical sequence to derive the overall project duration. The planned completion date is presented to the project sponsor who determines if the target is acceptable. If the planned completion date is not acceptable to the sponsor, a negotiation ensues, the sequence of project activities may need to be modified in various ways to tailor the project to the business required completion date. This can be done in various ways:

1. The scope of the project may be modified, including only essential features, and leaving certain enhanced features out entirely, or to be incorporated in a later release or process improvement.
2. The project team may identify activities that were initially planned to be executed sequentially but could be performed in parallel, saving on the overall project timeline. This approach will most likely add risk to the project, and this added risk needs to be conveyed to the sponsor. An appropriate decision with regards to managing project risks needs to be addressed.
3. Add resources to certain activities to decrease the time required to complete them.

In these last two scenarios, there may be an impact on the project budget which will also need to be communicated to the project sponsor, or may impact the planned completion date of other projects which utilize the same resources which have now been reassigned.

It should be mentioned here that realigning shared resources to shorten one project may not always negatively impact another project. Let's take a simple example of two similar tasks in two separate projects running in parallel (see figure 5.1). If we assign half of our resources to each project, the two projects will run simultaneously, starting together and ending together. Alternatively, we could put all resources on project A, and once completed, put all resources on project B. The total run time for the two tasks remains mathematically the same (and in reality, should be shorter!) The task in project B still ends at the same time as if the tasks run in parallel. However, the task for project A ends much sooner (figure 5.2!) This allows the shortening of the overall timeline for project A which can now move forward and complete earlier, without negatively impacting project B!

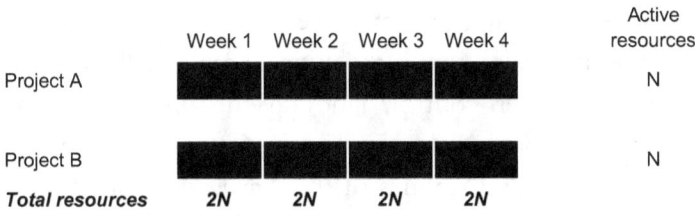

Figure 5.1: Resource allocation in parallel projects

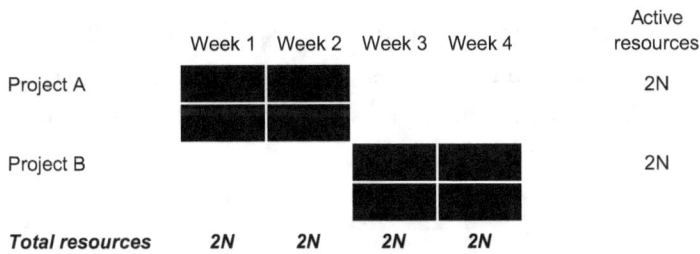

Figure 5.2: Smart resource allocation in parallel projects

The project's success or failure depends on the team's ability to complete the sequence of activities on time and meet the agreed target. However, in the *new normal*, there is a sharp focus on "what" needs to be achieved (scope/quality), but a hazy view of "how" that goal can be attained. Do you think an accurate schedule can be carved out upfront before commencing any project?

Maybe, Maybe not.

In the *new normal*, for some tasks duration can be determined upfront, however, others need guesswork. Guesses are made into assumptions and a series of assumptions are converted into project schedules. A software program creates this schedule based on the software algorithm, and produces a pretty 'critical path.' There is an illusion that if the critical path is delivered, the project is under control, ignoring the uncertainty and guesstimates behind the timeline presented. Yet some of the on-the-ground realities of the *new normal* work against the traditional deadline management approach.

The underlying hypothesis of deterministic time estimates is that those tasks that beat the time and cost estimates would be counterbalanced by those that finish late. In reality, while time overruns and delays accumulate, early completion and time savings seldom do! This leads to a strange formula

---

Time delays get passed on to subsequent stages but the time saved gets wasted before starting subsequent stages.

There are numerous explanations for why this strange formula is true. For one, as Parkinson's Law teaches us,

work expands to the available time and is often not delivered earlier than scheduled, even when completed!
1. Ample/excess time to complete an activity leads to procrastination, in favor of other activities.
2. Early completion of activity invites "gold plating." Even in cases where early delivery is achieved, the downstream resource meant to perform the next task may still be busy with their own previous task, and hence, is unprepared to take up the task early, effectively wasting any time saved.

Cost:

In normal times the cost of the project is derived by summing up the costs of all individual tasks.

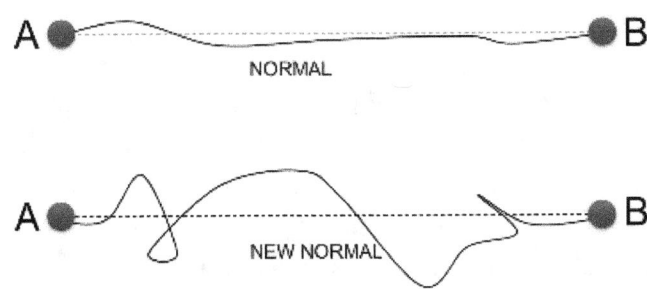

Figure 6: Shortest path to completion

Materials, human resources, equipment, and the methods or processes needed to deliver each activity successfully. In the *new normal*, cost estimates calculated upfront are seldom accurate. For instance, for going from point A to B in the picture, the normal effort is to minimize the deviations and to get to point B. Whereas in the *new normal*, it is not a straight path. This is not only because of higher unpredictability but also due to the iterations that have to be performed to successfully deliver a step as the very nature of the project which always existed. In the *new normal*, it is not only the people who come to projects with the masks, the tasks have masks as well. The lack of correlation between effect and effort also makes it difficult to predict the cost. Hence, do you think that controlling costs in the *new normal* is still feasible?

Maybe, Maybe not.

If execution time cannot be predicted precisely, and the scope is more precarious than in the past, the determination of cost will also be fallacious. If the initial cost calculation is misleading, the viability of the entire project comes into question.

Scope:

In the good ol' ways, the project scope is determined by including all of the requirements to deliver a project based on an initial estimate of those requirements. In cases of ambiguity, the scope statement is referred to, to see the demarcation between what is in-scope and what is out-of-scope. The list of assumptions, risks, and workaround options are all considered upfront. The scope also specifies who will have to bear the cost in case of a deviation. To avoid scope creep, everything needs to be correctly defined and identified at the initiation of the project. In the new ecosystem, where unpredictability is the constant companion of the project, do you think it is feasible to define a well-conceived scope upfront?

Maybe, maybe not.

Triple Constraints

In the *new normal* a sponsor may not be in a position to clearly and accurately define the scope of the project, knowing only the need of the market, but not exactly what is required to meet that need. With such a nebulous objective, the scope may only be defined loosely, needing further review and elaboration as the project advances. In fact, in some of my projects, I used to tell my people that the URS – user requirement specification - is known only when the project is finished and handed over.

> Changes will happen until there is no more time to change.

Instead of opting for an arbitrary scope determination and complicated change controls, why not define the underlying *purpose* in the first place?

There are numerous reasons why the upfront definition of cost, time, and scope may be more challenging in the new normal. Expecting the assessment of these three parameters to be static and unchanged from the beginning to the end of the project is wishful thinking and, frankly, unrealistic

The iron triangle model that we have been using for so many years taught us that achieving all three (scope, time, and cost) may prove elusive. However, having these three legs of the triangle in mind remains crucial so that we always remain conscious of the trade-offs that can be made between these three parameters, allowing us to choose between being faster or cheaper or better. That choice has all but disappeared. The *new normal* recognizes that time to market is of the highest priority, and if we can't be there on time, we really don't want the project at all.

Cost-effectiveness and high quality remain as project requirements, but as we have now prioritized time to market, these needs take on a different flavor. Providing a quality product or service to customers remains critical, but we can be more flexible as to whether we need to provide all features in the first-generation release, or if we can satisfy the market needs with a set of features that is good enough.

Remember, "good enough" is a very high bar! It does not imply inadequate quality in any way. It only implies delivery of a more focused product or service, that provides exactly what it purports to. Similarly, if there is no consideration of cost, the company will not show a positive return on investment, even in the medium and long term. Investment and cost of goods must remain in focus, but, not at the cost of late delivery, which will be even more disastrous to the company's bottom line. Products or services which are developed in such a manner reach the market faster or don't get there at all.

Yet, every crisis brings on opportunities that can be exploited

---

The rules which applied in the old good days are no longer applicable to the projects of the day.

Work hours

Prior to the pandemic "flex-time" referred to the hours in a day that an employee was physically in the office working. We recognized that while some employees needed to adhere to a strict schedule, e.g., shop floor workers, others, whose work was more individual, might work their hours from mid-morning to the evening, or come in for the evening or even the night shift. Of course, some companies were hiring remote employees who worked a day or two from home each week, but fully remote employment was rare and generally frowned upon.

Today that model has flipped on its head! With lockdowns, quarantines, distance learning, and social distancing, work from home has become the norm, and not the exception. People are moving out of population centers because they no longer have to worry about commuting times. More and more, companies are ignoring *where* their employees are located and are able to focus solely on the unique skill sets that each candidate can provide. Digital video and collaboration platforms have become an integral part of our lives and desktops. We have been enabled to operate in an unconstrained environment by unleashing the capabilities that modern technology has to offer in projects by enabling creativity and latitude to the time and space of work.

For the employee and organization alike this is a mixed blessing. Alongside the benefits of increased flexibility, travel time saved, and eliminating the aggravation of traffic jams, we see a blurring of the borders between work time and personal time. Working from home presents a multitude of distractions. With the office only as far away as the next room, we find ourselves working during hours that were previously dedicated to family time and responsibilities. Electronic platforms for communication have made us more efficient and forced us to adopt well-structured processes for managing t-cons and video conferences, bringing more focus to our working hours. At the same time to a great extent, we have lost the human connection and those semi-random interactions at the water-cooler and the coffee machine. How can the loss of "cross-pollination" and the resulting creativity of ad-hoc discussions in the hallways be measured?

The challenge in the *new normal* project is no longer limited to sailing the S-curve, but in beating the product lifecycle and technological obsolesce and getting a jump on the competition. Engaging the heads, hearts, and hands of the team and unleashing their talents in a dispersed environment is the right approach to achieve this. This can be accomplished by putting project ownership directly in the hands of the project resources. The environment is made more conducive so that they have a full sense of ownership. Entrepreneurial spirit and volunteerism are needed to carry out today's projects with full enthusiasm. An improved employee mindset will bring results, but superior results can be achieved only by inspired minds that are connected to a larger purpose. Businesses need to cultivate the inspiration and interest of the creative workforce of today while executing projects.

The dependency on man-material-machines has been shifted to people-innovation-ideas. Physical resources can be managed, but people and ideas must be inspired through exceptional leadership.

Triple Constraints

> *A project manager today is an unofficial counselor, psychiatrist, and motivator as well to the team.*

There is a stronger need than ever before for project managers to become true project leaders, as opposed to mere planners and technocrats. This is another not-so-subtle and very positive transformation happening within the project management fraternity. As projects depend more on cognition, creativity, and curiosity, there is a need for leading more and managing less.

Chapter 2

The Shift

For the *new normal* projects, the environment has imbued the classic triangle with a whole new perspective. There is a different view of the triangle which we call 'the opportunity view of the triangle.' By using the opportunity view we introduce a clarified and refined perspective. We believe that the conventional view of the triangle has been akin to observing projects through the wrong end of a pair of binoculars, and by suddenly turning the binoculars the right way around, allowing us a magnified view instead of a miniaturized perspective. When viewing every constraint as an opportunity we get the following:

Dimension 1: Time becomes velocity
Dimension 2: Cost becomes value
Dimension 3: Scope becomes purpose

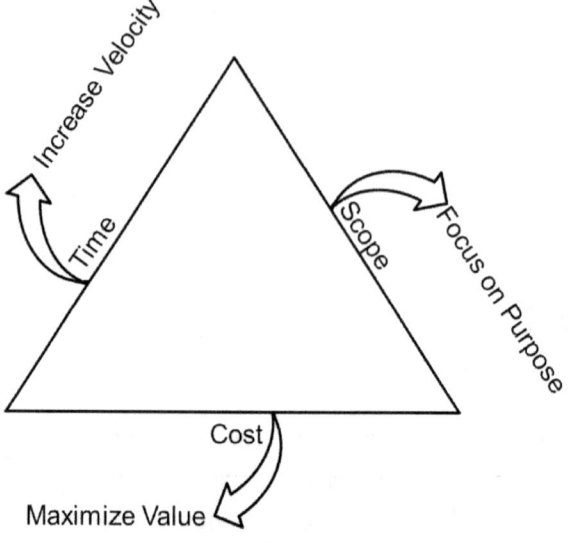

Figure 7: Unlocking opportunities

The idea behind controlling time (as if we could ever actually control time!) is to complete the project just in time, that is, just when it is needed by the company in the market, allowing the organization to assess commercial feasibility, time-to-market, and managing logistics, though not necessarily to complete the project at the earliest! Computation of a project schedule, not a simple task in the best of times, has become even more challenging in the *new normal*. For *new normal* projects whose goal is to meet the needs of the immediate crisis, perspective needs to be shifted to the speed of progress of the project, not only for the reasons already mentioned but even more importantly, to bring the project to successful completion at the earliest. Instead of controlling time, the focus shifts to increasing the velocity of each critical step. The speed of a critical step in the process must always be treated like a bottleneck in the project. Remember that in any system it is the bottleneck(s) that determine the capacity, or throughput of that system. Managing bottlenecks implies maximizing the speed through the bottleneck which translates to maximizing the speed of the entire project, which in turn, determines the overall project duration. This is exactly like a relay race, where the speed of each individual runner who holds the baton determines the speed of the entire team during his or her sprint. Increasing the velocity of each individual step is an opportunity to reduce the overall timeline. This, in turn, results in faster delivery. Moreover, phenomena such as *Student Syndrome* and *Parkinson's Law* can be avoided by focusing on improving the velocity of every critical step. See more on this in our discussion of project buffers, later on in this volume.

> ***Student Syndrome** refers to a tendency to procrastinate until just before the deadline of a project, which is caused, among other factors, by planning for excess time for task execution. **Parkinson's Law** states that the work expands to fill the available time which can be avoided by carefully controlling the time made available for each task.*

There are powerful yet simple techniques that can be applied to achieve this goal.

The logic of cost control is to ensure that the project is completed in the most cost-effective manner and within a pre-determined budget. Cost-effectiveness ensures that every penny spent on the project is worthwhile, and creates value for the client or sponsor. Instead of controlling the cost, the approach focuses on maximizing the project's value every step of the way. The dictionary definition of 'value' is the worth of all the benefits and rights arising from ownership. Creating and maximizing value can be accomplished in two ways: first, by increasing the *quality* of the product or service; and, second, by improving the *utility* of the product or service. Hence, the approach in the *new normal* is to look for opportunities for maximizing value every step of the way by creating more benefit to the customer for every dollar spent.

The principle underlying the concept of scope control in the classic sense is to ensure that the project and project team's objectives are aligned with the pre-determined purpose of the product or service being developed and to safeguard that there is no deviation from this purpose. In the *new normal*, seldom does everything go right the first time in a predictable manner, even more than before. When things do not go as expected, scope creep and change management come into play. A complex change control process, in turn, reduces the speed of the project and results in wasting even more resources through a cumbersome, time-consuming review, or worse, ad-hoc decisions that may not be fundamentally conceived, followed by the bureaucracy of the approval process. In other words, by following a *normal*, rigid scope framework, one sacrifices the flexibility that is needed when managing the circumstances of a crisis. Preparedness for unplanned tasks, harnessing emerging solutions, and responding to these occurrences in a lean and agile way is a key differentiator in the *new normal*. Rather than adhering to a rigid scope, maintaining the underlying principles implied in the project scope, in order to provide solutions for everchanging unmet needs is the shift that is needed. Laser-sharp focus on these principles helps the team remain adaptable and enables them to deliver them. Traditionally, this was ultimately achieved through scope creep management, so, being prepared for inevitable changes saves time by avoiding the bureaucratic change control processes that slow down the project's pace.

The only constraint a project has in the new normal is the opportunities it offers

There is massive potential for project teams to cultivate a new way of working by inverting the traditional approach; to improving each of these aspects (time, cost and scope) rather than merely controlling them. In the context of our current market instability, where there may be more unknowns than knowns, the ability to remain flexible will be a key success factor.

Wrongs versus rights

Traditionally project managers are those who consistently monitor the project in order to see that nothing goes wrong and to adjust when they inevitably do. They protect the projects and safeguard them. But a project manager of the *new normal* is someone who is focused on enabling positive changes to happen to the project and the team.

Project Management for the Newer Normal

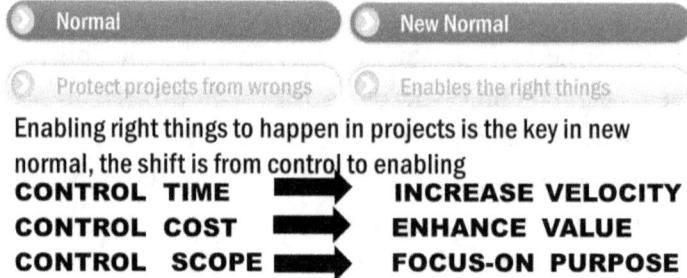

Enabling right things to happen in projects is the key in new normal, the shift is from control to enabling

CONTROL TIME ➡ INCREASE VELOCITY
CONTROL COST ➡ ENHANCE VALUE
CONTROL SCOPE ➡ FOCUS-ON PURPOSE

The command-and-control modus operandi are being shifted to inspiration and enablement. More than ever in the past, the project management role under the *new normal* is one of leadership.

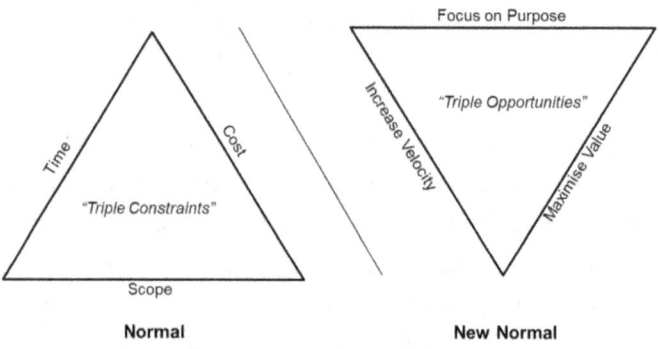

Figure 8: Transforming triple constraints

Time: Transforming deadline to velocity

In the past, the focus of project management was to work with the team to provide reliable timelines. The focus was more on reliability and predictability than on velocity. In attempting to achieve this level of reliability there was a school of thought that dictated padding the time allotted to each activity to ensure that there would always be sufficient time to complete them successfully, even when things went wrong. Paradoxically, the result of this approach was to lengthen the timelines of projects considerably, due to the reasons given in the previous section. Even worse, padding individual tasks failed to deliver the very reliability that it was meant to deliver in the first place! In the *new normal* the approach is not to master the art of controlling time, but to achieve an increase in the velocity of project progress. The velocity of the project can be enhanced with a variety of **accelerators**, such as monotasking, decentralization, clear and transparent processes, engaging internal and external subject matter experts, and reinforcing the collaboration between the teams.

Monotasking is one of the much-advocated methods stemming from the Critical Chain Project Management (CCPM) framework, in order to achieve full focus on critical tasks by each and every resource. The absence of distraction enhances the speed of execution – this is obvious. Monotasking helps in avoiding transition time between activities caused by attempting to juggle multiple activities and projects, reduces setup time, and accelerates the learning curve. This concept can be applied equally to a single resource or to an entire team.

Earlier we discussed that time saved is often wasted and that time lost is cumulative. Let's take this opportunity to take a deeper dive into this phenomenon, and remember that the concept of monotasking is critical.

Task mastery through constant single-tasking is another lever that can be used to boost the speed of execution. While monotasking and single-tasking tend to be used interchangeably, here we relate to them a bit differently. Monotasking is focusing and doing only one activity at any point in time. Whereas single-tasking refers to a *type* of task that a resource performs day-in and day-out repeatedly in order to gain mastery of that particular skill. This is something similar to the discrete manufacturing which Henry Ford introduced in the early 20th century. A door assembler in a car manufacturing facility attaches doors, day-in, day-out, forever. That single-mindedness allowed one to gain mastery in the 'art of door assembly,' and to become the most qualified resource in the world when it came to attaching the door to a car. Similarly, in projects we have people who can test, design, implement, project manage - when these people are allowed to do their one task, again and again, one after another, then they gain mastery in the execution of these tasks, and by doing so, eventually enable a reduction in time, decrease in errors and elimination of several iterations due to unnecessary trial and error.

Decentralization helps in gaining velocity of execution. Empowering the functions which execute the project helps them to make faster decisions, be agile and nimble in the development of the project, and reduce the complexity of communication. Decentralized project teams can benefit significantly in terms of having an unambiguous direction. This, in turn, results in the improvement of the velocity of the project.

The **process** in which the project team is enabled to work independently in order to deliver their part of the project must be clearly defined and well implemented. There are several such techniques available today, as the use of a **full kitting checklist** to ensure the readiness of a function to start their part before actually getting into the job.

Adherence to the full-kitting checklist avoids a premature start only to find oneself chasing after some of the prerequisite resources needed to execute the task seamlessly. Another example is the **stage-gate mechanism** which helps the transition of the project from one workstream to another seamlessly by ensuring that all pre-requisite activities are complete and the path is clear for the downstream stakeholders to take the baton forward and execute the project at the fullest speed.

Seamless **collaboration** between various functions that take part in project execution is a vital enabler of the increased velocity of a project. Improved integration between workstreams reinforces cooperation and interdependency. For example, if the design team works in a vacuum, they will likely propose a process that cannot be implemented by the fabrication team. However, having strong collaboration between the two functions will help to ensure that the design team is aware of the abilities and limitations of the downstream resource, and design a process that can be smoothly implemented on the very first attempt.

Cost: Controlling cost to maximizing value

Too much emphasis has been applied in many organizations to "save money at all costs!" It should go without saying that using a more expensive material, supplier or process is not always a waste of money. Consider that effective project management abhors wasting money or any other resource. However, if the premium paid means that significant supply delays or technical failures are averted, this is money well spent. We must always bear in mind that the first priority is to get to market! Once there we can work on process improvement and realizing efficiencies. In this way, we may not minimize cost, but we do create real value from each and every dollar spent on the project. Focus solely on cost-reduction, which ultimately costs time is, as the saying goes, "penny wise, and pound foolish."

The objective of the cost side of the triangle is not to make a cheap product. Instead, it is to bring about **value enrichment** in products and services which are to be delivered to the customer. The dictionary definition of 'value' is *the worth of all the benefits and rights arising from ownership*. This can be accomplished in two ways, by increasing the quality of the products or services and, by improving their utility.

Our approach to cost is to maximize value through each and every step of the process rather than to minimize expense. It bears repeating that time to market is paramount. "Saving" money on poor-quality components, materials and suppliers will often cause unnecessary delays and achieve exactly the opposite result. Once we have a product that meets the quality and utility needs of the market, we can introduce a new project to achieve additional savings eventually obtaining cost leadership.

Keeping this in the front of our minds, there are several **value enhancers** we might leverage in order to accomplish this goal. For example, there is a great temptation within project teams to deliberately add non-critical features to "add value", when it may be better not to add "gold-plating" to the first release of a product, saving these enhancements for a later release. This facilitates early market dominance which can then be sustained over time.

Similarly, discontinuing non-viable projects or features allows the focus of available resources on the core product technologies resulting in value maximization. Once a product is successfully launched into the market, a subsequent project may focus on process improvement or the introduction of less expensive materials or components to establish cost leadership. The objective here is not to compromise on the quality of the product but to deliver the project with the right quality through value maximization and continual improvement.

Maximize the value of each and every step, must start with clarity on what is '**nice to have**' and what is a '**must-have' feature**. When this is clearly held, it becomes easy for the teams to focus on the core purpose and deliver the same.

The ultimate goal is to deliver a product to the market and to do so as early as feasible. While it is tempting to work on advanced technologies it may be more effective to outsource these activities in the first instance in order to save time and to bring these technologies in-house at a later stage.

The other side of cost leadership is to look at **unwanted activities and processes** and eliminate them. Keeping all stakeholders and task owners aligned to best project methodologies and practices will avoid wasting valuable efforts and resources on activities that don't align with the **core purpose delivery**, consumes resources unnecessarily and waste valuable time in completing the projects. Recognizing this and removing it from the process improves cost leadership and is achieved by having effective monitoring and training processes.

The third aspect is to **add value** to the product or service at every step of the project. This starts by aligning to the core purpose, identifying opportunities for product differentiation, and performing value-added activities with the utmost efficiency. Improving the quality of delivery at every step enhances the quality of the project as a whole. Many times businesses suffer from initiating non-viable projects, that they identify only at a late stage, after resources and money have been consumed, never to be recovered. Taking cognizance of this and **pruning the failing projects** in a portfolio early enough, helps businesses to employ their cost and resources only on the projects which are profitable. Failing early is always better than failing later.

To achieve this there have been advancements in the risk management domain, which helps companies to identify problems early in the process. There are powerful tools such as the **pre-mortem** to identify risks and to manage them effectively. This also helps in eliminating or minimizing rework, which might be required. Rework is the result of poor planning or poor execution. Hence adequate forecast of risk through tools like the pre-mortem help in enhancing value. In research and development projects, rework until the final iteration are not going to add value to the product or services. Hence a thoroughly thought-out plan to minimize the number of iterations is something that adds value to the entire project and passes on the value to the customer.

The use of **outsourcing** to reduce cost and save time not only takes advantage of the expertise available elsewhere but also obtain services and use infrastructures more cost-effectively and more quickly trying to recreate them internally. The use of **cloud computing** is an illustrative example of this. Similarly, rather than waste valuable time in researching to reinvent existing know-how, the use of external **'subject matter experts** 'can save considerable time and add value and knowledge to the organization.

One of the best expressions I have learned about cost optimization is:

> *"Today's project teams have a lot of money to spend but none to waste."*

This is a profound message— we must invest every dollar in those tasks and activities that result in maximum progress of the project and, ultimately, in the improvement of value for the sponsor and for the end customer.

Scope: Rigid scope definition to purpose alignment

As we've already mentioned, the new normal business environment is characterized by a heightened level of instability as unexpected needs arise, seemingly out of nowhere. These unforeseen needs prompt businesses to react and respond rapidly to gain a first-mover advantage. These responses may take to form of small or large changes to the scope of an existing project. In the more extreme case, we find ongoing projects canceled and replaced by totally different project initiatives, to meet ever-evolving needs. This means that being prepared to pivot and adapt to these changes is a critical differentiator in the new normal.

This raises a huge new challenge to the organization, the burden of which is carried primarily by the project team and that challenge is, how can we be prepared for an unknown change that occurs at an unknown time? Our experience over these last months has taught us that such mental and logistical gymnastics can be achieved through an understanding that the project scope can no longer be seen in the rigid way that characterized our work in the past. Substituting "scope" for "purpose" in our minds can help to give us the mental flexibility that we need to allow us to deal with these changes in the fastest and most effective way. The moon mission is a well-known example of this. A laser-sharp focus on the objectives will help the team remain adaptable and able to deliver the desired outcome. This is not to say that we didn't experience changes in the past. We have always had to deal with scope changes as the external business and regulatory environment changed. We dealt with this by implementing cumbersome change control procedures that we can no longer afford. Being prepared for erratic change as an expected eventuality and adopting flexible mechanisms will help to avoid going through a bureaucratic scope creep/change management process that will only slow down the project's delivery.

The core purpose behind measuring scope is to ensure that the intended product or service the customer wanted is delivered in full as per the original promise. But there is a difference. Liken this to the story of the frog in boiling water. When the temperature is slowly and steadily raised, the frog continuously gets used to the slight temperature changes until it ultimately boils to death, however, when thrown directly into a pot of boiling water, immediately jumps out. Similarly, in times of stability organizations fall into a type of complacency and the impact of the time lost, though equally serious was, somehow more accepted by the business. But today, in the crisis-riven fast-paced world in which we find ourselves, the time lost has become critical with respect to customer needs, competition, and technology obsolescence. We now find on an all too frequent basis that the scope gets wholly changed from the time the project was initiated to the time when it is delivered.

How do you define the success of a project? Is it still defined by on-time completion, within the original budget, to the pre-determined scope? In today's context, meeting these parameters no longer guarantees the success of a project which must fulfill the very *purpose* of the project. Redefining 'success' as achieving the *purpose* and with no additional delay, and matching a sensible and agreed cost to the appropriate quality makes much more sense.

When it comes to purpose, it is essential to recognize the true customer of the product or service, and this may not be the project sponsor! The customer is the one who uses the end product or service created through the project. The sponsor remains the one who invests in a project intending to deliver and reap financial or other benefits. But it is key to define who the primary end-user is.

It is the customer who is the most important beneficiary of the project and more than anyone else it is the customer who defines what the true value is. If a project lacks the

customer's voice, the product or services it creates cannot be successful in the marketplace.

While the customer defines the purpose, the alignment of the team that executes the project towards this purpose is critical to achieving it. We call this the **true north orientation.** The purpose is the true north and the systems, procedures, and people are the resources working towards this true north. Remember you are only loyal to the true success of the project, not to anyone else.

The process which is used to reach the true north must be **change-tolerant** especially in this age of shorter product lifecycles, technology obsolescence, fierce competition, and high complexity. The agility to surmount obstacles and meet ever-changing product requirements will determine the success or failure of the project.

To cope, the process also needs to be able to **harness the creativity** of the people involved. There is much more innovation and out of box thinking required to solve the complex problems that projects bring today than ever before.

Customer's voice: The customer is the one who is going to use the product or service. If the product does not meet the requirements of the customer, it will not survive in the market over time. While market or regulatory dynamics may offer a short-term monopoly, today's free market seldom allows a monopoly to survive in any line of business for long. Hence, a project needs to be customer-centric, focusing on the need of the customer at all times. Having customers define the scope and expecting them to be a part of the testing is not entirely fulfilling the requirement. Following are some additional components of the customer's voice:

- Original scope definition
- Purpose of the product or services
- Regular reviews and stage gates
- Identification of 'must-haves' and 'nice-to-haves'
- Validating assumptions
- Testing and acceptance of the product

Customer input can, sometimes surprisingly, solve a complex problem that the project team struggles with. Hence, engaging customers in the journey of the project not only benefits customers but also benefits projects and project teams!

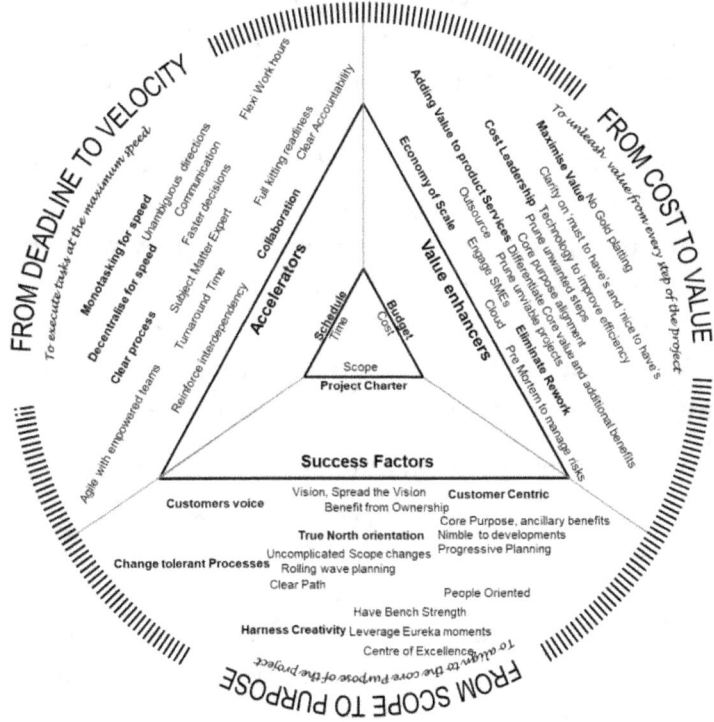

Figure 9: Levers of the Opportunity Triangle

A ready reference of the accelerators, value enhancers and success factors are as depicted in the picture. How many of them do we use in our projects? Following are some of the ways that you could get started.

GLOBAL BUFFERS

Buffers are the shock absorbers in a project to manage uncertainty. A buffer can be a time buffer, a cost buffer aka., budget contingencies, or a scope buffer.

Buffering the project, not the task is the key to minimizing the time to complete each task, and as a result, the entire project duration. As project managers, we've often been frustrated by projects being delayed over and over again by tasks not finishing on time. No matter how much time we allocate to a task, no matter how much "safety time" we build in, tasks take longer than our planning has allowed for. Human nature has much to do with this and as sophisticated project leaders, we must recognize the dynamics and help the project team to overcome some very natural human behaviors. It is our job, through respect, fairness and leadership to build the trust that enables teams to do their best and fastest work.

People are good and want to succeed. The first step is to understand and agree with the task owner what the duration of an activity "should" be 50% of the time, the median time to complete such a task, which is often called "50%-time." It takes a very high level of trust to get an agreement on a 50%-time duration. Trust that the resource will be allowed to focus on the task (monotasking) with all other tasks and distractions kept to a minimum, and trust that if there is any delay – and there will be delays 50% of the time – that they will not be punished for it! Thus, it is counter-intuitive for an experienced resource to commit to 50%-time. People want to succeed, to meet their commitments, not 50% of the time, but all of the time. So, when working with an experienced resource on how long a task should take, they will quite naturally build in "safety time" cushions so that they can have greater confidence that, even when things go wrong, they will still have plenty of time to complete the task according to their commitment. They do not want to disappoint the team, the project or the organization.

So, how much time should be added to a task to make on-time completion "more reliable?" In a normal "bell" or Gaussian distribution, how many Standard Deviations (SD) do I need to add to reach 65%, 80%, or 95% likelihood of finishing every task "on time?" With each SD added we considerably lengthen the duration of a task, and to reach even 80% "certainty" we need to add more than one SD to the estimated duration of the activity. What is worse is that we repeat this exercise for every single task in the project, even though we understand both intuitively and statistically that 50% of our activities ((by definition of 50%-time) will complete…on time, or even early! The other 50% will not and we have no way of knowing which tasks these are. So, what do we do? How do we know which tasks to buffer and which tasks to plan aggressively knowing that adding up all of the buffers for every single task in a project will add considerable time to the project!

As you may have already guessed, the answer lies in buffering the project, not the task. By allocating a buffer to the project, we can save at least 50% of the task buffers that would otherwise have been built in, considerably shortening the overall time to complete the project. Equally important is that when we see that a task is going to exceed the 50%-time allotted (as it will 50% of the time!) we allocate the additional time required with no sanction to the resource responsible for completing the activity. [Tip to project managers: encourage and work to on-time completion but **do not** punish the use of the buffer when faced with the inevitable. The first time you do, you will destroy the trust built up and it will be challenging to rebuild this trust!]

People are optimistic. The flip side of this is what is known as the *optimism bias*. In our world, we are witness to countless failures, and we enter into risky ventures all the time. Couples in love know that 50% of marriages end in divorce (in some countries in the modern era) yet they still go ahead and get married, believing that they will beat the odds and that their marriage will endure. They will not be part of the statistics. A project task is just the same. Although we have negotiated a nice comfortable buffer for our task, we truly believe that we will complete the task in the "normal" (median) amount of time, the 50%-time. Knowing we have plenty of time to complete, we procrastinate, we don't get right to it. Not because we are bad people or ignorant of the risks, but quite the opposite, because we believe in our own competence and capabilities, and believe that there are other, more urgent tasks to be completed first that demand our attention. Time gets wasted that can never be regained!

What if we had started the task immediately, despite having "plenty of time" to meet the committed date, and what if we completed the task in a timely manner (as we will 50% of the time?) Will this time savings be realized? Will it shorten the project duration? Here are just a few reasons why not:

- Will the downstream resource be ready for hand-off?
- What will management think of our overblown time estimates the next time? What does this do to trust?
- The task may be acceptably completed, but look how much time I have left to make it even better (gold-plating)

By committing to 50%-time we both set a realistic framework and create a sense of urgency to initiate activities when the task is scheduled to begin. The project manager is responsible to ensure that the activity leader is allowed to focus on that one, single activity so that it can be completed on time. We all know that there is a 50% chance that, even with full focus, the task will take longer than planned and when that happens a new estimate is made and time from the project buffer can be allocated to the activity. The downstream resources can be updated that the next hand-off to them will be delayed, and they can have their full kit in place, ready to start when the hand-over happens. In short, time saved in a task is now translated to time saved in a project!

Measuring buffer to measure delay is a very sensitive gauge of project progress or delay and can only be achieved by using a project buffer. We have many ways of estimating whether a project is on time. Some do it by tracking milestones, while others do it by sticking a finger into the air. Unfortunately, our optimism bias tends to skew our estimates, and by the time we realize that a project is facing a serious delay, it is too late to correct course, and bring the project back on time. Once we've created a project buffer, we have created a highly sensitive measure of the status of the project. CCPM makes use of what is typically known as a *fever chart*, which plots project delay against project progress. Every time we update our project, estimating whether any additional days of buffer need to be used, we can see exactly where we stand with respect to our project completion commitment. Should we move from green to amber or amber to red, we can make crucial decisions about how to get the project back on track, how to "regain buffer." For example, we may do this by reallocating resources to tasks that are taking longer than expected, or we may find that we need to increase risk by performing serial tasks in parallel, and then find a way to manage the increased risk. The important point to remember is that we can take these steps because we have a finger on the pulse of the project and we take full control of managing the project timeline, strategy and resources. You will rarely find a more powerful tool!

PROJECT VISION BOARD

Another simple yet powerful way in which the customer's voice can exist in the project is to interweave the purpose of the project into the vision board of all projects. The project vision is fully fused with the motives of the executing stakeholders. The shared vision is a critical factor of the project's success. Taking feedback from customers at regular intervals and selected stage gates and during project, review ensures the customer's voice is a dominant propelling force of a project.

> *Your brain will work tirelessly to achieve the statements you give your subconscious mind. And when those statements are the affirmations and images of your goals, you are destined to achieve them! - Jack Canfield*

Conventionally, once the project is identified, we move into planning mode. A key element that is often overlooked, or more likely, taken for granted in this process is to ensure that the objective is clear to all participants and in making this a shared vision of all players involved in the project. Getting into planning mode immediately after the project initiation is premature. Establishing a discrete task to create the project vision is essential. This has been recognized in Agile models.

A vision board is a tool in which the purpose of the project can be clearly laid out, and more importantly, is to be elaborated and maintained by the team which is responsible for delivering the project. Vision boards are a powerful visualization tool that conveys project objectives to the subconscious mind of the people who are executing them. The aim is not to add yet another document into already overburdened project documentation. Creating a vision board can be as much fun as we can make it. There are several ways in which the vision board can be created, but one of the major prerequisites is to have as many execution stakeholders as possible involved in this process. It is also critical to the process to include a regular review meeting with key stakeholders, including the sponsors and, to the extent possible, with the customers. Here are some ways in which a vision board can be created:

a. Mind mapping
b. Brainstorming session with the key stakeholders with post-its or flipcharts
c. A pin-up board in your office where you can pin pictures and printed statements.
d. Vision Board computer applications or mobile apps
e. Agile Vision Boards

My favorite process is to create a mind map. Mind mapping is a tool devised by Tony Buzan and is very much applicable for creating a project. One of my author-friends, Maneesh Dutt has written a book with the title "Mind Maps for Effective Project Management." This is a useful reference for the application of mind mapping into projects. Here is an example of a simple project vision board.

Project Vision Board

Purpose :	
Why This project Exist	

Customer:	Product/Service/Results Attributes:
Who is the actual customer of the project	What really the customer want (get to the core)

Business Goals :	External Factors :
What is financial, technical, strategic, capacity, competitive advantages of the business to undertake this projects	Competitors, regulations, customer, technology-obsolescence that affect the project

Milestones and Showstoppers	Key Constraints:
Delivery 1: Delivery 2: Delivery 3: Risk 1: Risk 2: Risk 3:	Drop dead date, Expertise, Financial Spent, Resources Limitations with which the project team need to work with

Figure 10: Project Vision Board

Following are some other important steps in order to create a vision board

1.   Get people to clearly understand and internalize the purpose of the project.

2.   Define clearly the customer needs and the value addition which the product or service is going to provide. This will become the overarching need for every workstream to refer to during project execution and facilitate decision-making in the spirit of the purpose.

3.   Identify clearly the people who are involved in the product including customers sponsors and other stakeholders and keep in regular contact with them.

4.   Define the business objectives and WIIFM 'what's in it for me' for each of the teams/team members involved in executing the project.

5. Define how it is going to be achieved.

6. Start weaving all these factors together in the way of a vision board. Be sure to include positive affirmations, energetic statements which can kindle excitement whenever anyone looks at it.

7. Make it visual - add photographs, charts, comments, pictures of the team members, numbers ($ and date), pictures of the customers. The more visual it is, the more connected it becomes.

8. Extend the project vision board to individual workstreams so that they can add their contribution to the project. While making the product vision board leave some space for people to add their passion.

The idea here is to convert an otherwise bland scope statement into an inspiring, well-connected vision board so that people can relate their role to the larger purpose. This vision board can be kept in the project corporate office and also can be kept in individual workstreams where people can extend it and apply it to their part of the project.

TRUE NORTH ORIENTATION

The purpose of the project is the true north of the project. Period. Every effort, system, process, and policy must be aligned towards achieving the core purpose. The purpose is the core benefit that a customer derives from a project to create a product or service. Everything else is an ancillary benefit that falls in the 'nice-to-have' category.

The purpose definition is to get to the very bottom of the requirement from the customer. The scope, decisions, and approach from the entire team are going to be aligned towards this. Only once the core purpose is defined, can timelines, decisions, and course corrections be taken in line with it. Fostering purpose-centric project ecosystems is an essential first step towards the attainment of true north orientation.

Progressive planning is a needed process in sailing towards the true north. It's like the captain of the ship making fine course adjustments to compensate for the weather while having a good plan for the journey mapped out in advance. Remember the managers we interviewed in the first section of the book? Those who said that there is no time for planning? Can you imagine getting behind the wheel of your car and driving without any information at all except for the destination? No idea how much gas is in the tank, the road or traffic conditions at that time of day? Whether you need to pack some food for the journey and what clothes to take? I think we now understand how mistaken those managers were – especially in the *new normal*.

Rolling wave planning (a more illustrative term to describe 'progressive planning') is an excellent 'middle way' which allows time for a fundamental map of the journey to be drawn up and is much more useful and efficient than trying to create an arbitrarily and over-detailed initial schedule. The finer details dictated by reality cannot be planned with any accuracy upfront, and if they are, will surely be heavily modified as interim goals are achieved. Progressive planning is exactly the methodology to be implemented to achieve the most effective and efficient results.

This is not to say that the main activities and interim goals cannot or should not be planned up front. If we look back to our sea captain, embarking on a journey from India to Europe, we know that he will carefully plan out the route and sea lanes that he will use. It only means that we cannot foresee every eventuality at the beginning of the voyage, and we know that course corrections, small or large, will certainly be needed along the way. If suddenly, the Suez Canal is blocked by a ship running aground, as happened quite recently, the captain needs to decide whether to wait out the delay at sea or decide that it may still be faster and cheaper to circumnavigate Africa to save time on the way to the desired destination.

In short, for activities in the foreseeable future, we would be well served by a detailed project plan. Activities coming over the horizon should also be planned, but not in extreme detail. Only as these activities come onto the visible planning horizon would we add in the more granular detail of the activities required.

The benefits of planning progressively are multiple. First, we save a lot of redundant planning time when we recognize that specific activities planned too far in advance will likely need adjustment later, so why waste time with granular plans that are, at best, theoretical. Second, as we do begin to visualize these downstream activities, it is important to identify and plan the specific activities required, so that adequate preparation, such as full-kitting can be applied early enough to avoid delays.

The team needs to be prepared to be agile and flexible in light of happenings during project execution. The bottom line is that our processes need to be **change aware** and **change tolerant**. The complicated scope change process, comprising endless documentation to rectify and consolidate scope creep is not an efficient mechanism to serve the purpose of today's projects. Furthermore, all too often these processes serve only as an excuse for project delays or budget reconciliation. Either way, it is not a healthy addition to the client–business relationship. Adopting an **uncomplicated scope change process** including a flexible master plan and high-level budget which can be refined using the same principles of progressive planning can be much more effective to deliver the purpose of the project.

Harnessing creative energy is needed and it is people that are the most critical factors and resources in a creative process. The agility and flexibility to adjust to changing project intricacies require creative problem-solving skills. Capturing and implementing **eureka moments** not only facilitates creative problem-solving but also pumps up the energy of the resources which are involved in project execution. In fact, having a strong and deep bench capacity helps in adaptive planning as additional resources are needed to address challenges as they arise. Allowing people to develop excellence is a key success factor more than ever before, and this reinforces centers of excellence (see 'Single Tasking') within the business. This can only happen when our processes are people-centric.

The Missing Process

The project team works diligently to create products, services and deliver results. Traditionally, the team would report on whether the project is behind or ahead of schedule. Thus, project progress is measured in terms of time or percent completion, rather than the purpose it is set to achieve. How many tons of earth have been excavated? How many doors have been installed? This world view focuses the mind on minuscule tasks rather than on the value being created, which is the very soul and purpose of the project. There is a tendency to choose the clock over the compass.

Successful projects are navigated using both the clock and the compass.

Another observation in the traditional teaching of project management is that effort versus time indicates there is less effort and resource consumed during the early and late stages of a project. The maximum resources are expended during the execution of the middle of the project life cycle.

Think again

The process that is often missing is "setting the shared vision" of the project even before the first task is executed. Setting a compelling vision with stakeholders is a vital success factor in the new normal. Thinking back to our example of the Apollo mission to the moon, projects with "blank checks" succeed because of the intense vision, larger than any one individual or team involved.

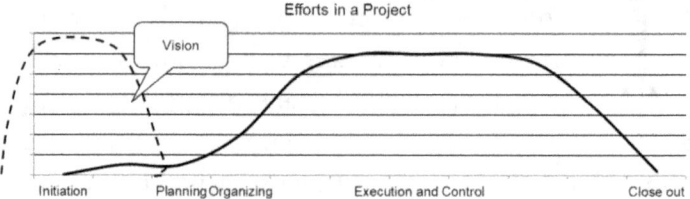

Figure 11: The missing process

While traditionally the clock helped project managers sail towards on-time project delivery, the true north or attaining the ultimate goal plays a significant role in the new normal. The application of design thinking and OKR for measuring project success helps a project manager to balance the clock with the compass.

Four fundamental shifts organizations must undertake to get to the new paradigm

INCULCATE DESIGN THINKING

Design thinking is a problem-solving methodology that can be applied to a wide range of problems, from designing a new product to developing a business strategy. Design thinking can also be applied to project planning. The design thinking process typically includes the following steps:

Empathize: The first step is to understand the needs and experiences of the people who will use the product or service. This involves talking to users, observing their behavior, and getting to know their motivations and challenges. This step is critical for ensuring that the design addresses the real needs of users.

Define: The next step is to define the problem or opportunity that the design will address, based on the insights gained from empathy. This involves synthesizing the information gathered in the empathy phase and identifying the key problems that need to be solved.

Ideate: In this step, designers generate a wide range of ideas and potential solutions to the defined problem. This can involve brainstorming, sketching, and other creative techniques to explore different possibilities.

Prototype: Once designers have identified a few promising ideas, they create rough, low-fidelity representations of the most promising ideas in order to test and refine them. This can involve creating physical prototypes, digital mockups, or other forms of representation that allow designers to get feedback on the design.

Test: In the final step, designers gather feedback from users and other stakeholders on the prototypes, and use this feedback to refine the design. This can involve user testing, focus groups, or other forms of feedback that allow designers to iterate on the design and make improvements.

By applying design thinking principles to project planning, teams can create plans that are more user-centered, innovative, and effective in achieving their goals. The process helps to ensure that the project is focused on solving the user's problem, and that the project plan is flexible and adaptable to changes in user needs and other factors.

OBJECTIVE AND KEY RESULTS

OKR stands for Objectives and Key Results. OKRs help project teams to focus on what really matters, and to measure progress towards achieving their goals. OKRs can be applied to projects in order to provide a framework for setting goals, tracking progress, and ensuring that the project is aligned with the organization's overall strategy. The following are some ways OKRs can be used in projects:

Defining project objectives: The first step in using OKRs for projects is to define the project objectives. Design thinking can help in evolving with specific, measurable, and aligned projct goals. These are qualitative statements that define what the organization or team wants to achieve. They should be challenging enough but achievable and should inspire and motivate the team.

Setting key results: Once the project objectives have been defined, the next step is to set key results that will measure progress toward achieving the objectives. These should be specific and quantifiable and should be achievable within the timeframe of the project. For example, key results might include metrics such as the number of new customers acquired, the amount of revenue generated, or the number of product features delivered. Every result can be driven as a sprint as explained in the Relay Race model in subsequent chapters.

Monitoring progress: Throughout the project, progress toward achieving the key results should be monitored and reported regularly. This can be done using project management tools or other reporting mechanisms. By tracking progress toward the key results, project teams can quickly identify areas where they need to adjust their approach or allocate more resources to achieve their goals.

Adjusting goals: If progress towards the project objectives is not on track, the project team may need to adjust their goals to stay aligned with the organization's overall strategy. This could involve redefining the project objectives, revising the key results, or changing the project scope to achieve better results.

Overall, OKR is a useful framework for setting goals and tracking progress in projects. By aligning project goals with the organization's overall strategy, project teams can ensure that they are making progress toward achieving their objectives, and can quickly adjust their approach if needed.

AUTOMATION, DIGITALIZATION, AND MACHINE LEARNING

The use of technological advancements to benefit the project and its processes is becoming ever more essential as a key success factor. The new normal requires people to work from remote corners of the world, and reliance on digital technologies is inevitable to share information and communicate in the new challenging ecosystem. We are all experiencing digital enablement touching our lives in many and varied ways. Unfortunately, in project management, we are not seeing the level of advances that might be expected and much more progress along these lines is still required to create seamless systems and processes efficiently. There are countless helpful project management applications available in the market, if you are still just using excel for project planning, think again.

ADAPTIVE PROJECT MANAGEMENT

Deterministic models helped early industrial-era projects. In the new normal, the more adaptive the governance is, the better for the project. In some industries, information technology, for example, an Agile approach helped reach adaptive goals. For more highly regulated industries it may be presumptuous to think that the same benefits could be reaped, and a more adaptive or progressive model, incorporating some Agile principles, as appropriate, might be a more practical approach.

Is it the end of the story?

Not Yet

Adapting our project processes to the new normal already looks like plenty of work, doesn't it? Is there a framework that factors in all of these aspects in order to deliver projects successfully in the new normal? The answer is yes, and that comes with an attractive metaphor. We look forward to exploring that framework in subsequent volumes.

Part II:

The Methodology

The Methodology

Fastest man in the world, Usain Bolt set the world record in the 100-meter dash in Berlin in 2009 when he tore through the tape and the previous world record in just 9.58 seconds. When Bolt teamed up with three more runners to run the 400-meter relay, each of the four running their respective 100 meters, they achieved a record time of only 36.84 seconds. For those of you reading this and doing the math in your heads, the average time to run 100 meters in the relay was less than Bolt's world record; only 9.21 seconds! Individually Bolt set the fastest time in the 100 meters. Collectively, Usain Bolt's team was faster in the relay beating the fastest sprints ever run by any human in the 100-meter dash to date. If Bolt was a project manager building a Gantt chart for the 400-meter relay, he himself would never have imagined, that he along with his team would be able to accomplish this. Bolt's own best individual performance in the 400-meter run is 45.28 seconds. The enhancement in performance was made possible by dividing the 400 meters into discrete 100-meter segments, allocating the resources to each segment, and bringing out the best in each of the team members in performing their roles. What can we as project managers learn from this common sports example and apply in our profession?

We love project teams, and a project team that is focused and motivated is truly a thing of beauty to watch. Seeing a

The Methodology

great team in action reminds me of those slow-motion films of a thoroughbred racehorse in full gallop, grace, and perfection, poetry in motion. Project teams work exceptionally well, particularly when approaching deadlines. When in a race against a project delivery target, a good team can beat all previous records and meet even the most aggressive of deadlines.

Human potential is tremendous, and when correctly aligned with a larger mission or project and nurtured by a conducive ecosystem, normal or *new normal* incredible results are possible. So, why is it that we are so surprised on those all too rare occasions when everything does work exactly (ok…mostly) according to plan? Why is success not the norm to be expected and relied upon throughout a project and across all projects?

Divide and Conquer

Like in the 400-meter relay race, where we allocate each 100-meter segment to a different runner for enhanced performance, a project in the *new normal* also can be divided up into several smaller sections to deliver the goal effectively. The key is to set the vision clearly and plunge into action without any further delay.

How to eat an elephant? In Small Pieces!

Traditional management philosophies held that a manager had to be an expert in all of the fields of knowledge and endeavor of the employees reporting to him. In the new reality, we have come to recognize a different reality in which it is increasingly unlikely that any one manager can be the master of all he manages. Today's managers inevitably work with teams that combine the knowledge of many different disciplines in order to achieve their objectives. The master-builder approach in which one omniscient visionary reigned supreme is as relevant today as Edison's first phonograph in the age of the iPod.

The intense level of project complexity in the 21st century is rooted in the increasingly multidisciplinary nature of the *new normal*. The high level of sophistication dictates that projects be executed by experts from diverse fields and can no longer be completed by a single person. In our increasingly specialized world, there are domain experts to perform each part of an assignment. Take, for example, software development; we have client-facing teams, developers, testers, and more. In addition to these functional roles, there is a management team that consists of project leaders and a team leader. Each of these specialists is trained and has developed the core competencies to perform their respective tasks. They are capable of learning or inventing the technologies required to create a groundbreaking product and to do so at the speed necessary to complete their respective tasks in time to meet market needs. These subject matter experts are best qualified to solve problems and offer technical alternatives should course corrections be required because they deal with the same type of work day in and day out. Their ability to provide creative alternatives within their areas of expertise will be far better than that of a generalist who may not have the same depth of knowledge or degree of experience. It is essential to take the best of these domain experts to achieve the best results of the project.

This brings us back to our relay race metaphor. The coach plays different roles which are nearly in conflict with each other. On the one hand, his ultimate responsibility is to drive the team to cross the finish line in their best possible time, and he must never lose sight of the big picture. However, he achieves this by focusing on the fine details ensuring that each member of the team has everything he needs to deliver his very best efforts from acceleration up to receiving the baton, running his best race, and finally slapping the baton in the hand of the next runner.

The role of a project manager in the new normal is equivalent to the racing team's coach. He must never lose sight of the finish line, for if he does he may steer the team in the wrong direction.

At the same time looking at a project only as a single massive endeavor will not enable the individual teams to focus on the true urgency of tasks at hand and to deliver them as fast as required. It is exactly this dual focus of accomplishing each task to the full scope and on time without losing sight of the big picture and the relationships and interfaces between the different activities that are the key to project success. We have a need in this *new normal* to shift our approach towards seeing a project as several interconnected, interdependent mini-projects, we can successfully achieve a larger purpose. Mini-projects consist of rapid execution cycles which are unambiguous to drive, and several intermediate successes can be obtained at regular intervals which executing larger projects. There are, in fact, multiple benefits to working this way in addition to faster project completion.

> *Hence, in reality, a project includes several 'mini-projects' which are performed in parallel or one after another in order to deliver the overall objective of the larger project.*

Treating a project as one massive monolithic effort has the following issues which we will learn to address using the mini-project approach:

- *A massive monolithic project is complicated to manage effectively.*
- *One starting point and one endpoint result in one kick-off and only one success per project, at the end.*
- *A project is planned as a single endeavor, the planning, execution, and control processes will assume a 'one size fits all' approach, whereas several workstreams may be involved in this process and each needs his or her own environment in order to perform their activities effectively.*

Having a single time point as a goal tends to encourage the "rubber-band effect" which is in conflict with good control of intermediate goals.

Quality checks may not be performed frequently enough and may be performed considering final objectives without sufficiently focusing on intermediate deliveries, which are critical to deliver robust products, services, and results. If a project needs corrections towards the end, it is far more time-consuming and costly to travel back in time to correct an error made upstream.

When a project is identified as a failure, it is often recognized too late, as most of the resources and cost might have already been incurred. Managing a single large project does not allow making course corrections early enough.

Chapter 4

Deconstructing a Large Project

A large project consists of various stages, which are delivered one after another or in parallel in order to create a product, service, or result. Projects are progressive, and various aspects are only revealed during project execution as activities are completed, and the project progresses to the subsequent phase. This is an inherent characteristic of any project and particularly of complex *new normal* projects. The degree of progressive unfolding varies depending on the type of the project, but for all projects, there is an element of uncertainty. For a simple brick-and-mortar project, we would expect to find relatively few surprises as we proceed. However, for a complex and highly innovative project, we would expect to encounter more problems requiring creative solutions and to find them more frequently. Regardless of complexity, we would make our project estimates right up front, during the planning phase. The time required, budget, resource deployment plan, and communication plan are all worked out at the beginning of a project when it is not yet fully elaborated or even fully understood. This lack of detail can be only partially compensated for by making "guesstimates" based on past experience. So, it should come as no surprise that most projects deviate from these original estimates. These forecasts, no matter how accurately calculated become effectively irrelevant the moment the project begins.

Ironically, in practice, project planning is done upfront at the time when our estimates can be made with the lowest level of accuracy.

As the project unfolds, visibility of the real project tasks, timeline, and costs needed to deliver the project increases. This, in turn, results in assumptions, buffers, and plan B's in order to ensure that the project teams can try to recover from any eventual drift from the initially estimated scope, budget, or time commitments. The diagram below illustrates the inaccuracy of current estimates which is represented by the dotted line. At the beginning of a project, estimates are highly inaccurate and become more accurate as the project progresses.

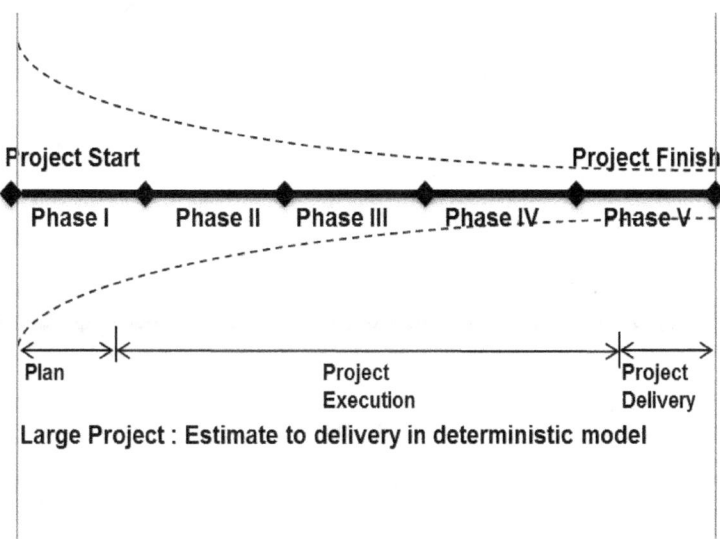

Figure 12: Forecast inaccuracy in a project lifecycle

With the benefit of hindsight, all commitments would be perfectly accurate. Unfortunately, we only gain this wisdom once our activities are completed, or at least, nearly so. We can turn this to our advantage if we turn the graph around. We have the best visibility and forecast accuracy for those activities which need to be performed in the near term, at the beginning of a project. We find that we only begin to deviate significantly from our original planning as we progress with our project. Hence it is obvious that the possibility of a project to stick on to the initial estimate can be higher at any point in time rather than determining upfront.

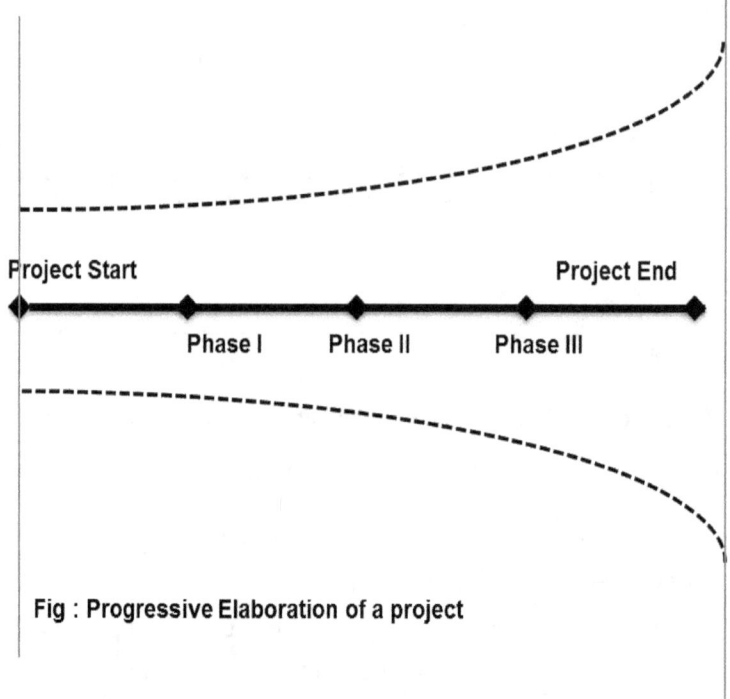

Figure 13: Progressive elaboration in a project lifecycle

Even the best estimates that are forecast at the beginning of a project become irrelevant very early on. As the project begins, the dynamics change, assumptions become reality, and the pre-configured plan becomes obsolete even before the first phase can be executed.

> *Large projects are more vulnerable and have higher chances of failure than small projects.*

Think about it mathematically. Every single task in a project has some probability of being delayed or failing simply due to predictable variability. If you add to this the known and unknown risk factors related to each task the probability of success decreases further. The overall probability of the project finishing on time is the product of the multiplication of all of these probabilities. Thus, the more tasks in a project, the higher the likelihood of failure. One way to mitigate these factors is by employing mini-projects. In a mini-project, the level of focus can be intensified, and the mini-project gets delivered quickly. Predictability is higher in smaller projects.

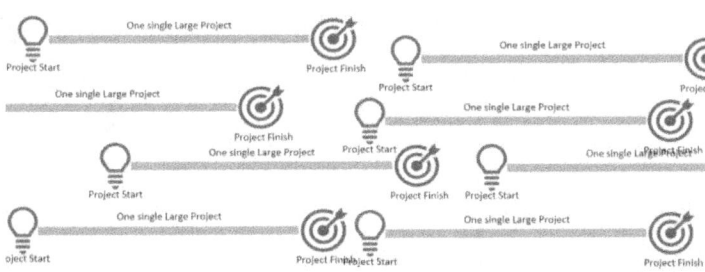

Figure 14: Large projects in a multi-project environment.

Need for Mini-projects

> *"If you cannot do great things, do small things in a great way."* - Napoleon Hill

We cannot do without the large projects which are necessary in order to create meaningful products or services. How would the Hoover Dam have been built, or the Airbus A-380 aircraft without being able to manage large projects?

A large project is co-created by multiple domain experts each with their respective area of competence. Each domain expert has a role to play, and the output from each one can be seen and managed as a subsection of the larger project. In this book, these subsections are referred to as mini-projects. Every mini-project is performed by an individual subject matter expert or a team of experts working in that domain who have the required knowledge, experience, and insights about that particular section of the project. The following are the primary reasons why a *new normal* project could benefit from being governed as mini-projects:

Project Phases: Every large project has various phases which need to be completed for the project to fulfill its ultimate purpose. Each of these phases has nuances that need to be dealt with. However, each of these phases needs to be treated uniquely to get the maximum advantage from the respective domains. In software development, for example, the phases are analysis, development, test, and release. Each of these phases is performed by team members coming from different disciplines each having its own intrinsic characteristics and nuances which must be recognized. Mini-projects will ensure that the project manager treats each segment as a small project in its own right which provides an opportunity to address each discipline on its own terms to bring out the best in each one.

Specialization: The master-builder era existed in the Industrial Age or before when all projects depended on an individual architect or engineer who, as the name implies, was master of every aspect of the project at hand. In the 14th century when a castle or cathedral needed to be built, it was the master-builder who was responsible for everything from the design and construction of the fortifications, to the artistic carvings on the doors. In the *new normal*, every field has exploded with its own specialization and super-specialization. An excellent example of this is the medical field. Initially, physicians were generalists who could treat all ailments, at least all those known at the time, using the treatments available. Now, medical science is divided into specialties and

Need for Mini-projects

subspecialties for every different ailment and body part. Not only do we have oncologists, cardiologists, neurologists, and surgeons, but we also have surgeons who specialize in performing very specific procedures. This amazing progress in medical science has paid high dividends in the improved precision of diagnosis and treatment of disease or injury. There is an increased probability of success of every surgery compared to the general surgery of just a generation ago.

The same holds true in the business environment. There are planners, programmers, testers, business analysts, engineers, scientists, quantum mechanics, and quality teams, each of them needs to execute their respective project tasks. Scientists are organized according to their field of expertise and managed in professional departments that specialize in subject matter like discovery, basic research, development, analytical chemistry, and physics. Similarly, engineers are classified according to their own domains like mechanical, industrial, civil, or electrical. This specialization helps in delivering the best expertise in the respective field and improves the efficiency of executing an individual task. Individual tasks, collectively increase the efficiency of the overall project. Specialization allows each expert to keep up with the latest trends, employ the most updated technology and access the best insights and knowledge in his or her respective field.

As we have discussed, many of today's projects are more complex than the old normal era. To adequately address this complexity and to deliver innovation in an increasingly competitive market, extensive knowledge in diverse spheres is required. Let's look at smartphones, for example, in the highly competitive consumer electronics market space. Each and every feature of the new device must be thoroughly considered and planned when designing the next models. For the latest smartphone to compete a developer must consider such dissimilar aspects as materials of construction, battery life, optics for the camera, audio quality and software for the operating system, as only a few examples. Each of these disciplines is a universe unto itself and requires a team of experts to plan and design the respective parts. If that were not complex enough, the whole thing has to be delivered within ultra-strict size and weight specifications. Mini-projects is a practical mechanism by which we can bring out the best in each specialized project team and facilitate fast and effective project delivery.

Outsourcing: Businesses source many components and services from external suppliers, partners, or contract research or manufacturing organizations. Outsourcing allows each company to focus on what they do best, and to buy the components and services from others when this competitive advantage is absent, or merely inconvenient.

Outsourcing facilitates economies of scale and allows efficiencies to be achieved at each step across the value chain.

Take, for example, an automobile manufacturing facility that has an assembly line fitted out to assemble new cars. The facility will have thousands of manufactured components that are not manufactured at the facility itself

Need for Mini-projects

but are made and supplied by external parts makers, each expert in manufacturing the respective parts. The same happens in a project environment. Many sections of a project may be outsourced, be it manufacturing or research, programming, or testing. There are even projects that outsource close to 100% of their activities, but we are not referring to these here. Consider instead a large project in which in order to save time, money or both, the project manager chooses to buy certain components rather than to produce them internally, even if the expertise is available to do so. Many of the software development projects outsourced to India today are typical examples of this type of outsourcing. In pharmaceutical product development projects, outsourcing clinical trials is also a similar example. Original Equipment Manufacturers (OEMs) are crucial to the success of many capital projects. The outsourcing of these components needs to be managed just as any other individual entity within the project as the entire operating framework, resources and, procedures are unique. Applying the rule of the master builder is not necessarily the most effective way to achieve success in such sections of the project. Employing the mini-project philosophy to these activities as well ensures that procurement of these key components will get the attention of its own planning, follow-up, and control mechanism.

A notorious example is a battery developed for the Galaxy Note 7. This outsourced component turned out to have devastating safety issues which caused this "state-of-the-art" smartphone to overheat and even to explode. This fault was only discovered after the product was launched globally. Airlines were not allowing the phone aboard their flights even with the phone turned off. This single snafu in product design had a catastrophic impact on Samsung's share price, which at one point had lost 19 billion dollars and cast a harsh shadow over Samsung's future smartphone business. While overall the product had superior features, the failure of this one single outsourced component, threatened the entire viability of Samsung as a player in the smartphone market. This example well illustrates just how critical it is to have rigorous control and management focus on every aspect of the project and that a lack of focus on outsourced components mini-projects would make the larger project vulnerable and even lead to disastrous outcomes.

Global Scale: Wouldn't it be great if our project teams could all be located in one place? We could all sit in one room together to plan and coordinate projects, resources, and activities. We wouldn't have to consider different time zones, working hours working from home, or national holiday schedules. We could get together at the coffee machine and informally brainstorm ideas.

Geographical differences matter and while we may not like to believe it – believe it! Every country and sometimes state or even city has its own employment laws, dialect, cultural makeup, and its own unique way of thinking and behaviors. It takes different approaches to motivate teams in different locations to deliver their best results. Similarly, two different sites which are considered to have identical equipment and materials may find that a process that works robustly at one site, delivers a very different product at the other and I can tell you from personal experience that this risk is very real and happens more often than you would like to believe. Unfortunately, in the globalized world in which we live and operate the management, design, and technical teams may be scattered all across the globe due to the location-based capabilities inherent in the modern, industrialized economy. Different aspects of a project may be carried out in different locations, and there may be no single place where the entire project team ever comes together. Since there is no one single set of rules which applies globally across all project segments and all territories, it follows that every part of the project which is executed in a different geographical area will abide by its own set of rules. Again, we see the benefit and applicability of the mini-projects approach. One development site is driven by end targets? Another site works best when following a plan that is highly detailed? Yet a third site works every other Saturday? All these can be adequately be accommodated by implementing mini-projects which makes it impossible to err by assuming a one-size-fits-all mentality. Likewise, adjusting for differences in management framework, leadership style, and motivational aspects which can always be found to some extent between teams are automatically accounted for when considering each of these project sections as mini-projects of the larger project.

Large Project Schedules Are Full of Assumptions. It's hard to prepare an accurate plan upfront for all project phases. For complex projects which require creative and truly unique solutions, the classic techniques for predicting timelines and forecasting costs are seldom an easy or accurate endeavor. Consider a complex project that requires a significant number of experiments to be performed before a robust product and process can be achieved. Due to the nature of the project, it is unknown just how many iterations it might take before success can be achieved. In such a scenario, since we don't really know how long the project may take it is often easier to rely on the execution team to self-manage this section of the project instead of trying to come up with accurate time, cost, and scope estimates for this segment. Consider a technology-driven company that is right on the cutting edge of its field. It is not unusual to find in such a company that it not only allows but requires the technical team itself to propose the scope, costs and target completion date for the core technological aspect of a project. In these cases, it may be the same expert team that is responsible for defining the objective and to develop the technology; that is responsible for estimating and meeting their own timelines, set and meet their own budget, and deliver a product in full, to their own high-quality standards. This is often needed to be worked out as a mini-project. Several such mini-projects constitute a larger project.

One Size Does Not Fit All: Every phase of a project has its own nuances. The rules we follow when creating a project plan for one phase of a project may be totally inappropriate for the next phase, and so the rules need to be adjusted to meet the needs of each project phase. One example of this is from my life as a project manager in pharma, though I know the same general concepts apply to other disciplines as well. The early phase of a project is performed by a dedicated R&D team with a known pool of resources, and any clash of resources that may occur between projects can be resolved by senior R&D

management. Once the process has been developed by the team, the project is handed off to the production team for implementation in the plant. Plant teams have a multitude of responsibilities, only one of which is the development project. There is no local management function that can prioritize these competing activities. Similarly, the R&D culture has a very different sense of urgency than that of the typical manufacturing unit. Thus, assuming that the way projects are planned for one domain (development) is the same as the way projects should be planned for another domain (manufacturing) is not a valid concept. We know up front that our project plans need to include the manufacturing phase.

> *We also know that project management software is not intended to nor is it capable of managing a manufacturing operation. Yet, we still tend to use the same project management tools to plan for and manage the manufacturing plant stage of the project.*

Wouldn't it be better to adapt our planning tools and approach to match the project environment? Similarly, the speed, agility, efficiency, and value-add would be different for a business, a researcher, operations, quality, a developer, or the testing laboratory team who are engaged in the various sections of a project. Hence, treating all of them the same way does not result in achieving the best overall efficiency of the project.

Autonomy: The *new normal* workforce consists of an ever-increasing proportion of Millennials who are driven more by the need for autonomy than previous generations. Make no mistake; it is still important to ensure that they have a clear direction and understand management expectations. However, once the rules are clear, this is a generation that resents being micromanaged, and appreciates the freedom to operate, with a passion for delivering results, ahead of schedule and with the highest standards. The more complex and creative our projects become the more these traits become an advantage allowing them to find solutions and drive innovation with new ideas. We need to find the right balance to avoid stifling these younger employees with too many rules, regulations, and glaring oversight.

Cognitive Nature:

> *You are not managing the projects that were managed by your manager. Applying the yardsticks which have been useful for your manager is not necessarily applicable to your projects.*

The *new normal* projects are more cognitive in nature as compared to the projects of just 15 or 20 years ago. As such, a greater proportion of project time is dedicated to learning and reflection in preparation for project planning than in the last generation. Business growth is driven by those projects that bring true innovation and can convert technical innovation into new products, solutions, applications, software, artificial intelligence, and biotechnology. These are not the brick-and-mortar projects of yesterday and should not be managed as if they were. It is not the construction of a building, which requires more brawn than brain. Today's projects require more power of the mind to stay ahead of the curve. A mini-project allows the most qualified expert to focus on a single problem to be solved unleashing the very human and creative intellect in order to deliver the desired outcome best.

Industrial Revolution and Projects

The industrial revolution resulted in a paradigm shift in the manufacturing segment, but projects, as a domain did not catch up with the movement. When Henry Ford introduced assembly lines and discrete manufacturing, many criticized him for it. Ford's initiative was, arguably, the first introduction of a mass-production system which resulted in extreme throughput, continuous flow, simplicity and ultimately resulted in faster and much more efficient production of the 'Model T.' Until then, there was a team that manufactured the car as a whole; even today we have companies that manufacture each car as a distinctive masterpiece one after another. However, Ford envisioned a new and unique concept. He identified and isolated several tasks and embedded them in the assembly line that manufactured or assembled each section of the car. The worker who assembles a car door assembles them one after another, and that is all he does. The door expert develops mastery in the "art of door assembly". The precision and quality of his door fabrication become superior over time as he focuses only on the perfection of door building. In fact, no one else can assemble a door of the quality of this craftsman nor can anyone else be as efficient. Another benefit to this type of specialization is that Ford ensures that each expert has available all of the tools and materials that he needs to complete his discrete task so that he need not be distracted from it by chasing after the right bolt, wrench or knob.

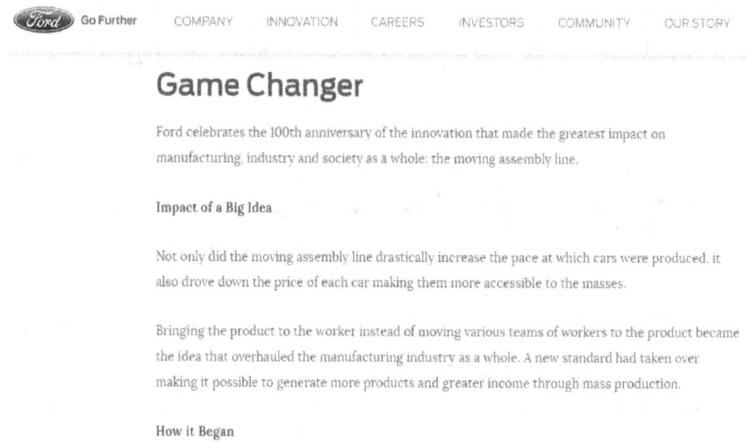

Figure 15: Ford's assembly line concept as in their website (http://corporate.ford.com/innovation/100-years-moving-assembly-line.html)

Once Ford's assembly line was established it didn't take long for industrial evolution to revolutionize the way in which products were manufactured through mass manufacturing facilities everywhere. The Japanese honed this concept with quality circles, also known as kaizen, which encourages like-minded specialized workers to share their challenges and together to find better ways of working and best practices. These initiatives resembled and led to, lean, continuous improvement and six sigma.

Manufacturing operations are refined bit by bit through continuous improvement and to the extent of achieving quality levels exceeding 99.99% defect-free. We can evidence this from industries such as automobiles. The Kaizen initiatives are a way of life in this segment, where process imperfections are identified and corrected continually, and productivity is increased.

It is quite amazing that with a well-refined, validated process that is known and needs to be repeated as exactly as possible as long as a product is manufactured to the given process, we can get 99% efficiency in the manufacturing department. In contrast and despite the great success in the manufacturing sphere, projects, which are unique by their very definition, suffer from success rates hovering around 60%, and some estimates are even lower. These dismal statistics are published by prominent Project Management Institutes (Institute, 2018), the proponents of project management, so you can imagine what the naysayers believe. The reason for these bleak outcomes is that adoption of high-performance techniques and methodologies of project management is still quite low. Some improvement which has been achieved in projects has been due to the introduction of project management software and other hi-tech equipment to replace manual labor. Still, projects are often treated as large endeavors as was automobile manufacturing done before Ford's assembly line concept.

The concept of continual improvement which is so important in production processes and in quality assurance has not been embraced in the project's domain.

Considering resources as experts in their area and having domain experts driving the projects is still quite rare. This is not without reason. Traditionally, projects by their definition are temporary endeavors with a definite start and definite finish. There may be some scope for having a team come together again to perform a similar project and to benefit from harvesting the learnings in a subsequent project. However, project teams tend to be created and disbanded upon completion of a project. Subsequently, as a new project comes along, a new project team is created from the resources (experts!) available at that time. It is not usual to have the same project team to continue the same projects continuously, and it may not be critical in the case of large construction projects for megastructures and brick and mortar projects. However, today's industrialized companies are far more sophisticated and understand that a single project's success, while providing new sales and improving business performance is not sufficient to ensure ongoing robustness. Rather than evaluate or work on one project at a time these companies are concerned with the promotion of a whole portfolio of products and services to be offered to the consumer. These concerns continuously evaluate new projects to be added to the portfolio where each project is considered both on its own merits, but also as part of a strategic vision where the entire portfolio is worth more than the sum of its parts. Many of these complementary projects may be similar in nature or, at least, share some high-level similarities. The desired result might be the delivery of several related products and services or several versions of them. The workflows of these projects will remain similar or at least have identical elements and areas of expertise even though the products, services, and results remain unique.

One caveat here: No two projects are ever identical, by definition. Having said that, there are sometimes projects that may appear to be so similar we are tempted to copy the development plan of one project and only modify it in a few places to create a new project plan. If we have numerous projects that all appear to be quite the same, with only a relatively few differences, we may even be tempted to create project templates for use in all of these projects, each with only small modifications. My years in project management have taught me that the use of templates in project management is a mistake of the penny-wise-and-pound-foolish type. Sure, you may save a few hours, or even a day or two when building the initial project plan from a template, and you may believe that you have identified all of the places where the projects differ from the template. The fact is that in any complex cognitive project, even two that look quite similar, the use of a template stifles the thought processes of the project manager and the project team developing the project plan and, ultimately, the project itself. A project that is worth doing that will cost significant resources in time and treasure is worth the extra few hours that it will take to create the project plan from scratch.

What can be done? If templates are "bad" practice, what is "good" practice? After all, this may not be the first project that a group planned and executed, and we certainly cannot afford to ignore the lessons learned from previous project experience. What can we learn from the advancement and improvements in manufacturing during the industrial revolution and how can we apply them to today's projects? We have already discussed why it is not good practice to copy the same boilerplate from one project to the next, so, what is good practice and how do I apply all of my learnings and expertise from managing one project to managing another?

Just as there are experts in assembling car doors on the Model T, there are expert groups who focus on each aspect of project management and execution. Experts in project planning will meet with each subject-matter expert (SME) or group to understand all of the tasks required to be performed and the interrelations between each of the tasks. The planner will work with the team to understand the time and resource allocation that the team foresees to create the plan with the help of the appropriate software and planning tools. With that plan created the planner can then confirm whether the plan meets the business objectives with respect to the delivery time and budget, and if necessary, re-work the plan to meet those objectives. Meanwhile, project risks need to be identified and mitigation plans put into place. Just planning the overall project-at-large can be seen as a mini-project in its own right, and that mini-project will be managed by a project planner who has the required expertise and experience.

Each separate workflow, which will be executed by its own SME or team of SMEs is in turn built by the planner. These

Industrial Revolution and Projects

SMEs and their mini-projects may include design, development, and testing, for instance, which are a widespread practice in projects. Each expert group is seen as a contributor to a part of a whole project, and the project has only one finish line. Just by splitting the projects into several mini-projects and providing the same level of autonomy, allows these groups to develop and to employ their learned expertise similar to that of the assembly line workers who have become experts in their own discrete realm of manufacturing. Their focus, efficiency, and expertise can be improved progressively as they move on from one project to another.

Following is the comparison of operations and projects

Parameters	Operations	Projects
Variability	Variability exists, but to a lesser degree as performed repeatedly	Highly variable
Certainty	Relatively certain	Highly uncertain as performed for the first time
Predictability	High. Improves through predictive maintenance	Low. Progressively elaborated. Some projects are iterative
Challenge	Variability	Uncertainty
Result	Same product, one after another	Unique products, one after another
Tasks	Well defined	Progressively elaborated

Success ratio	99.99966% yield, 0.00034% defect, Six sigma level	68% met original goals 58% completed in budget 52% completed on time (PMI, 2018)
Scale of Operation	Mass manufacturing	The scale is not mass in many projects, the possibility of several similar 'kind of projects' in programs and portfolio.
Techniques	Same practices Well established processes Refined to the core, Continuous improvement	Similar workflow Every project is unique. Only follow a process flow of initiate, plan, organize, execute control and close out
Repeatability	Repeatable with standard operating procedures	Recreate every time, as each project is unique.

While it is not fair to compare operations and projects, there is a vast opportunity for projects to inherit some of the approaches which operations deployed in order to improve the project performance to the next level to a meaningful success rate from 60%.

Chapter 7

The "Art side" of Projects

People never want to be part of the process, but they want to be part of the outcome. the process is where you figure out who is worth being part of the outcome - Unknown

Project execution is both an art and a science. Unfortunately, we seldom consider the art of project execution when attempting to improve the speed of project execution. Art and creativity are well recognized as playing a legitimate role in research and programming, and even in such apparently technical practices such as testing or costing of processes yet, somehow the art is not seen as an enabler to improve the efficiency of projects.

The art side of anything is developed over a period of time. While it is not easy to define exactly what we mean when we talk about someone's art, we all know it when we see it. There are renowned artists today and throughout history who mastered their fields of endeavor through observation, trial, and error and through experience. Anyone who goes to the museum to view a Monet or a Van Gogh can appreciate the quote

> *"Great things are done by a series of small things brought together"* - *Vincent Van Gogh.*

Their mastery seems uncanny, or at the very least, some unnatural intuition or talent. As we study the art more deeply, we begin to discern some technique or pattern, and over time we can understand them better. Meanwhile, the artist is using his intuition and talents to expand and deepen his art. Similarly, in projects, SMEs specialize in a specific domain. They hone their skills over time through observation, trial and error, and experience. The experience develops into intuition and as they learn more intuition is eventually developed into a science. Since every project is unique, we require the SMEs to take responsibility for the aspects of the project closest to their realm of understanding. These SMEs are best equipped to handle the science as well as for those aspects not yet fully elucidated; these same SMEs are still best placed to solve a conundrum empirically and theoretically. For each domain, we have the respective domain experts to execute each of these sections / mini-projects. By enabling the art side can benefit the people as well as projects.

The Japanese, for example, keep their teams intact for a longer period than the duration of a single project. Each participant knows their role, and he or she performs in accordance with that role. This creates synergies within the team and develops process maturity, increases speed and reduces variability in the projects. While it may not be feasible to have a Japanese-style team in every part of the world, we can attempt to understand the dynamics and to adopt the best practices that can then be applied to projects. This is possible by splitting the projects into discrete functions and enabling the relevant expert group to work in their respective area. There are four significant benefits of enabling this.

1. Reduction in variability
2. Increasing speed
3. Reducing the 'MUDA' or waste
4. Enhancing process maturity

Reduction in Variability

There are several types of variability in a project. The variability could occur because of the uncertainty of the task. When different stakeholders commit to a project, each has their own way of working. When the projects are executed by people from across the world, each of the territories has their own culture, which gives rise to another aspect of variability in the project. When a project is performed by multiple teams including outsourced partners, this naturally causes a lot of variability in the way of working. The larger the project, the bigger the team size, and the more extensive the geography, the more variability will creep into the project.

VARIABILITY DUE TO CHANGEOVER There are setup and transition times while switching from one project to another. When a person changes over from one task to another or one project to another, there is an element of transition between the two activities, introducing variability. The transition from one task to another, from one person to another or one team to another team also brings in variability. This is because no two tasks are identical, and no two teams or even two people work exactly alike.

By focusing expert resources on those activities that they do best, we decrease the number of different people performing those activities, and we decrease the assortment of activities performed by one individual resource or team, and as a result, we can use the principles of the relay race to decrease this source of variability

VARIABILITY DUE TO FALLING OUT OF RHYTHM The productivity of a resource, whether equipment or human, may vary depending on the 'state of being' of that particular resource. For instance, an instrument that is well maintained would result in fewer failures and better throughput than a poorly maintained instrument. Similarly, a human resource who is a key enabler in today's projects would tend to produce better results if they were in good health and good spirits, demonstrating a strong identification with the team, ownership of the project and accountability to the organization.

THE INHERENT VARIABILITY OF A RESOURCE

When people are engaged in similar types of activities, that are closely related to each other and performed in proximity to one another, there is a rhythm that develops, and the work tends to flow with an uninterrupted elegance. This is the objective of mini-projects; enabling people to do what they are really good at and keeping them engaged in what they are passionate about with few distractions by other types of tasks, for example. The rhythm created enhances performance. When an individual is required to perform multiple and diverse activities, seemingly at the same time in some chaotic dance of multitasking, he runs the risk of falling out of synch as he switches over from one kind of task to another, and that introduces variability in his performance. The rhythm of doing develops once sufficient familiarity with a process is achieved while these similar tasks are performed repeatedly.

This is the objective of mini-projects; enabling people to do what they are really good at and keeping them engaged in what they are passionate about with few distractions by other types of tasks, for example. The rhythm creates an enhanced performance. When an individual is required to perform multiple and diverse activities when he switches over from one kind of task to another, he gets out of sync, and that brings in variability in his performance of two different sets of tasks. The rhythm of doing things develops once the consistent process is performed over and over again.

VARIABILITY DUE TO PROCESS INCONSISTENCY Lack of clarity in defining and streamlining procedures that are performed routinely causes people to attempt to figure out unique and more efficient ways of accomplishing the same task every time. This inconsistency leads to variability in time, effort and quality. Conversely, a regular and repeatable process, executed, the same way every time, would improve efficiency and provide excellent results. In summation, a process that is ad-hoc and inconsistent is a recipe for a high level of variability in performance and quality.

TRAINING VARIABILITY Typically, we find that many types of activities are performed by groups or teams, and not by individuals. Each member of the team may be responsible for similar tasks and may be considered to be interchangeable with one another. However, we have all experienced that situation where we have a job to be done, and we prefer that it be done by a specific individual ("no one but Jack touches my car!"). This may stem from a number of factors that lead to mastery of a task and our trust in that individual. One key element in gaining such expertise and trust is through rigorous training, as well as various motivation and accountability factors. We've all experienced that the same task performed by two different individuals may have different outcomes be it the quality, the reliability or the speed at which it gets accomplished and training and mastery are important contributors to the variability.

COST VARIABILITY There is more than one solution to most problems, and even the same solution may be implemented in more than one way. The solution itself, as well as the mode of implementation, may bring to cost variability. To illustrate this, consider that you got to your car to find that the air was low in one of your tires. You go to the gas station and fill all your tires with air to the prescribed pressure, but lo and behold, 2 days later you notice that the same tire is looking a bit flatter than the rest. You go back to the gas station and fill the tire and now that the leak is confirmed, you need to take it to be repaired. One repair shop insists that the tire needs to be replaced, at the cost of $150, while another happily finds the screw lodged in your otherwise healthy treads, pulls it out and patches your tire at the cost of $15. In both cases, you no longer have a flat tire, but at very different costs.

CREATIVITY AND COGNITION The relay race methodology is enabled through the utilization of the most expert resource in a discipline to perform each relevant mini-project or task, reducing variability and increasing familiarity. It is important to understand that these guiding principles hold true even when the project is highly creative and requires ingenuity and inspiration. You might reason that complex projects which require a high level of inventiveness and originality would not fit the model of specialization and familiarity, so remember that everything is relative. Relay race does not breed out creativity and ingenuity. Consider a project that does not resemble anything that has been done before it. It may not even be known where to start. Relay race simply tells us to use the most appropriate resource to do the exploratory work in order to map out what we know and what we still need to learn in order to proceed. Once we believe we know in which direction or discipline to find the solution, utilize the SMEs with the best expertise to develop the technology and drive to the desired solution.

Increasing Speed

Our overall approach is that we benefit when we can reduce the time to deliver a project. This is achieved by executing the critical activities in the shortest time possible. The relay race approach to achieving this goal is to break the large-diverse tasks down into smaller, more specialized activities that can each be performed by the most qualified expert. The time to execute the project is reduced by implementing a variety of accelerators, including monotasking and specialization, clear and transparent processes, use of subject matter experts, and having good project coordination to facilitate the collaboration between the teams, all increasing project speed.

Monotasking is one of the most important principles of the relay race and when implemented strictly reduces distractions and enables heightened focus on the part of the resources. This focus enhances the speed of execution of each task by every resource executing his activity and, ultimately the project. Monotasking helps in avoiding the transition time while juggling between multiple projects, avoids setup and reset time, and enhances the knowledge curve. Task mastery through continuous monotasking is the lever that can be used to boost the speed of execution. SMEs can plan, design, test, implement, and project manage. When these people are allowed to specialize, they gain the utmost speed of performing each task

> *A second key element of the relay race is the decentralization of authority. This means the empowering of the expert teams to make independent decisions with respect to finding solutions for and the execution of their own tasks.*

Faster and more effective decision-making by the expert team will result in good technical decisions and decreasing the time of execution. Decentralization also reduces the complexity of communication within the team and between teams with adjacent activities. Decentralized project teams are better at maintaining clarity of mission and keeping on point. This, in turn, results in fewer errors, less need for rework, and improved project performance times.

Full kitting is a third important element in ensuring the success of relay race. The concept of full kitting is to ensure that all required documentation, materials, and equipment are available before starting an activity. A good recipe for getting stuck in the middle of an activity is to rely on the fact that whatever you don't have yet will magically and reliably appear "on the fly." In addition to ensuring that the team does not get stuck in the middle of performing a task because they are missing an element, they need to complete the task, just the creation of the full kitting checklist helps to ensure the readiness of a function to start their part before initiation of the job itself. Ensuring a completed checklist avoids wandering around searching for some of the prerequisites while wasting time and putting the task itself at risk.

In a relay race run in an athletic competition, one of the most important elements is ensuring a seamless and well-timed handover of the baton between one runner and the next. The timing of the handoff and making sure that the runner receiving the baton takes his head start on time and is ready to receive the baton is the coach's responsibility. Precisely the same is true in our relay race metaphor of project management, and it is critical that we ensure that the transition of a project from one function or team to another is well-coordinated and seamless. The implementation of phase reviews is vital to facilitate this. It is the project management team that plays the role of the coach and is responsible for the seamless transition of the project from one work stream to the next. The phase review is to ensure that all prerequisite activities are complete and clear path for the downstream stakeholders to be ready and able to grasp the baton and continue to carry it forward through project execution with the fullest speed. A clear understanding of the true unbuffered turnaround time of all activities and transparency to the downstream teams, in particular, is crucial to ensure that they exactly what to expect and exactly when to be ready to receive it. Seamless collaboration between various functions which take part in project execution is a crucial enabler of increased project speed.

Reducing the 'MUDA' or Waste

The concept of MUDA refers to the consumption of resources with no value being added to the project or to the portfolio of projects as a whole. MUDA teaches, for example, that a machine or an employee standing idle is a waste. However, the relay race concept of project management takes a different approach. One way to think about waste is to consider what resources are required in order to ensure that we can effectively complete our project in the shortest time and at the lowest cost. Coming back to our classic relay race competition as our example, think about what we observe as the race is run:

The starting gun fires and runner number 1 accelerates off the block and begins running his 100 meters towards runner number 2.

Runners number 2, 3, and 4 are waiting in their positions. Would anyone say that runners 2, 3 and 4 are just standing idly by and wasting resources?

As runner number 1 nears runner number 2 and the end of his sprint, runner number 2 needs to start accelerating. He may start his acceleration as much as 10 meters before the baton "exchange zone," which itself is 20 meters long. Thus, he may run a redundant 30 meters in total to get up to maximum speed while receiving the baton. Were these 30 meters of effort wasted?

Meanwhile, runners 3 and 4 are still waiting in place for their turns to run. Are these still wasted resources?

The handoffs from runners 2 to 3, and 3 to 4 are essentially repeats of the handoff described in point 3 between runners 1 and 2, so the question of wasted energy and resource repeats as well.

Admittedly, none of these idle or redundant resources are wasted at all, but rather the resources are required to be in place in order to finish the relay in the shortest time possible. Moreover, in projects, while the first runner is doing his lap, the third runner would be engaged in the third lap of another project before he gets on to the subsequent project. In a way, these small breaks between projects are necessary to gain traction and to another project. This is advantageous than juggling between multiple projects at the same time. In this way, we can refine the MUDA definition if we say that we create maximum value with the resources available.

Another aspect of eliminating waste is to eliminate rework. By perfecting the running, acceleration and handoff techniques we also minimize the likelihood of the baton exchange going wrong. Just imagine that if instead of a good sturdy slap into the palm of the next runner's hand, the baton went flying and then rolling in the grass or on the track. Then you would surely see redundant activity, and no amount of effort in the world would ever get that team to cross the finish line first.

In these ways of ensuring excellent procedures and coordination between team members and by making sure to keep resources available when necessary, even if kept idle (!) true waste is minimized, and cost leadership in new project delivery is achieved.

There are several value enhancers we might leverage in order to heighten cost leadership which is implied in this model. We must not go around gold plating our efforts or activities but only do as much as required to reach a good enough result. Runner number 2 will only overlap exactly the number of steps required to reach maximum speed for the start of his own 100-meter run. There is no glory in running more than he needs to and tiring his sprinting muscles too early, or in other words, less is definitely more.

As guiding principles ask yourself these questions:
Are you decreasing overall project time/time to market?
If the answer is yes, it is a good bet the resources expended are a bargain.

Are you decreasing risk significantly?
(Note: the product of probability times impact is the way we qualify our risks.) Probably a good use of your resources. Think about your auto insurance policy. You never want to use it, but you wouldn't drive your car without it.

What is the impact on quality?

There are additional opportunities to attain cost leadership adding value to the product and services and proactive definition and elimination of risks and reworks. The objective here is to not compromise on the quality of the product but to deliver the project with the right quality through value maximization

As a prerequisite to maximizing value, it is critical to have a clear plan and understanding of your project. A clear understanding of the scope of the project right at the outset is crucial and especially identifying what attributes are must-haves and those that are merely nice to have. Furthermore, for each task, and certainly for each phase, section or mini-project, you need to understand which activities must come before others, and which activities would be nice to have before others. Armed with a clear understanding of the "must-have" vs. the "nice-to-have," it becomes easy to manage every step effectively and to correct when things don't go according to the original plan. This clarity allows the teams to focus on the core purpose and to deliver it. While the temptation to gold-plate is very human and may never disappear completely, a clear understanding of the scope will help the teams to avoid this tendency and in delivering the best value proposition.

A more difficult step, but no less necessary for achieving cost leadership involves challenging our paradigm of how to work. Are all the planned activities really necessary, or is it just the way we've always done things? As our teams become more focused and gain even more experience in the specialization, a natural outcome of mini-projects, they should be able to identify and avoid redundant activities that were once thought to be indispensable. With renewed value analysis of your project methods and practices, you may surprise yourself by what activities may ultimately be revealed to be redundant, freeing up resources and decreasing the time to complete a project. Recognizing our own short-sightedness and identifying the requisite process improvements will help drive cost leadership.

Before ending this section, we would be remiss if we did not take a giant step backward to gain a bit of perspective beyond the individual tasks, mini-projects processes, and procedures. The project as a whole, both in its own right and as a part of the greater portfolio must also be considered when looking at budgets and considering cost leadership. Knowing when to stop a project and stop "throwing good money after bad" is every bit as important as knowing how to choose a good project for the portfolio. During the life-cycle of a project, many things may change, either internally or externally. Externally we may see a change in the number of competitors, or in the conditions or the needs of the market. Internally we may find that delays in execution of the project, or unexpected requirements or workarounds mean that crucial launch deadlines would be missed, or that the remaining cost of the project is no longer justified by the expected revenues.

Continuing to work on a project that is not of sufficient value may be the most wasteful use of resources of all. This must and can be avoided through good governance, for example, using a periodic project review process. The project status is reviewed including the time and other resources remaining to complete the project as well as revisiting the relevance of the business case that justified the project as of the last review. The earlier a project that will not bring sufficient value can be identified and canceled, the sooner we can stop wasting resources that would be better spent on projects and activities that will bring value. Furthermore, the expenses at the early stages of a project when the scale is small are generally also small. The farther along we progress, the higher the costs become. If we can identify a "bad" project and cancel it in the early stages of development, the money and other resources lost should be small relative to the project budget. In today's hypercompetitive business environment, resources are always limited, and we do not have the luxury to waste them on projects that do not justify their use.

One important caveat is that it is very tempting to look at how much money, time, or effort has already been invested in a project when deciding whether or not to cancel it. This is what accountants call "sunk cost" and considering these costs is one of the big mistakes we see managers making when considering whether to continue or discontinue a project. The resources expended, I am very sorry to say, are never coming back. Looking back in regret is not a valid business proposition. Only looking forward and asking ourselves whether it is worth utilizing the remaining resources estimated in order to gain the potential value from the project is valid in making this crucial decision. Taking cognizance of this and pruning the failing projects in a portfolio helps businesses to focus their budget and resources on those projects which are the most profitable. Failing early is better than failing later.

The "Art side" of Projects

Enhancing Process Maturity

The use of the mini-project technique, especially when used over time helps to improve process maturity and achieve synergies between teams throughout the organization, while also making roles and responsibilities vividly clear to all.

HANDOFF As a project progresses from stage to stage, the metaphorical baton is passed from one team to another. While there may be room for some flexibility or variability in the way two different teams perform an activity, this is not true of the handover process. The handover process is a critical activity, and even slight variation could cause the baton to be fumbled. Thus, the handoff process must be especially well designed and understood in order to ensure alignment and continuity as the activities move from one team to the next.

ROLES AND RESPONSIBILITIES When a task is delegated to a team, and the objectives are understood with absolute clarity, the level of performance can be expected to be much higher than if the objective of the task is not clearly and precisely defined and understood. This may seem as obvious as saying that rain is wet, but it does bear mentioning here simply because of the importance, and the fact that it is all too often taken for granted. Activity leaders must be completely aligned with the desired outcome of the project and understand how the task they are performing fits into the schema of the overall objective of the project. Ambiguous guidance that does not explicitly define acceptable results leaves too much room for individual interpretation which may not necessarily be in line with the direction of the project and is a recipe for failure.

ESTIMATE ACCURACY

While there are many important dividends paid by the relay race methodology, this is surely one of the biggest. Whether at work or at play, youngsters and oldsters alike, every single one of us has asked and has been asked: "how long is that going to take?"

On the one hand, we "suffer" from what Prof. Tali (Sharot, 2011) describes in her 2011 book, *the optimism bias*. Simply stated, this means that we tend to be optimistic about the outcomes of what we are doing. This bias is extremely important, which is why it has survived the evolutionary process and significantly contributes to our motivation to go ahead and attempt something new and, often, risky. If we believed we were set up for failure, we probably would not spend our time and efforts engaged in a Sisyphean endeavor, would we? The optimism bias causes us to estimate optimistic net durations for our tasks, as we believe that we can finish them in average time or less.

Conversely, we all want to be reliable. It doesn't take too much life experience to learn that no matter how diligently and enthusiastically we may embark on a task, there are countless other demands on our time that often cannot be avoided. (Just one second, the phone is ringing again…ok,

The "Art side" of Projects

I'm back.) As a result, we tend to add cushion, because we fully expect that there may be numerous interruptions, all very important, no doubt, and we don't want to disappoint anyone by missing the due date that we committed to. How reliable do I want to be? 80% reliable? 90%? Just think of how many standard deviations it takes to cover 90% reliability! The cushion can be very amply upholstered indeed!

So, optimism bias, on the one hand, cushioning for reliability on the other, which estimate is more accurate? This variability is one of the most fundamental reasons that projects are so often delivered late. Mini-projects performed by specialists who are focused on a single task or domain will result in more accurate forecasts because this is what they do all the time. Perhaps even more important, since they are focused on one area of performance, they are naturally faced with fewer distractions and, hopefully, less inclined to multi-tasking, which is the biggest enemy of efficient task completion. Using the SME estimates for mini-projects will allow their greater experience and focus to provide realistic estimates for each project stage and for project managers to better estimate the overall duration of a project. When repeatedly performed, not only do estimates become more accurate, but the net duration actually starts shrinking as a result of learned expertise, focus, and monotasking.

PRE-MORTEM

Advancements in the field of risk management help organizations identify the potential problems in a project earlier. Powerful tools such as the pre-mortem help to identify risks and to manage them effectively prior to the project or even before every mini-project. Pre-mortem is a method first coined by Gary Klein in his article in Harvard Business Review. The teams pretend that as if the project has already failed and work backward for the reasons for the failures. This yields the real challenges and potential pitfalls in a project and helps the project teams to work out preventive approaches to overcome these before it happens in a project.

> *A premortem is the hypothetical opposite of a postmortem. A postmortem in a medical setting allows health professionals and the family to learn what caused a patient's death. Everyone benefits except, of course, the patient. A premortem in a business setting comes at the beginning of a project rather than the end, so that the project can be improved rather than autopsied. Unlike a typical critiquing session, in which project team members are asked what might go wrong, the premortem operates on the assumption that the "patient" has died, and so asks what did go wrong. The team members' task is to generate plausible reasons for the project's failure.*
> *(Klein, Sep 2007)*

Any tool that helps us to envision potential pitfalls will help us avoid them, or at least to be ready with mitigation plans should we encounter them along the way. Doing so helps in eliminating or minimizing any rework saving valuable time and resources. Rework is the result of poor planning. Research and development projects are often iterative by their nature and can be an art as much as a science with some amount of trial and error involved. Still, proper planning and design of experiments can streamline the process and minimize the number and extent of experimental cycles required to reach the desired outcome. A thoroughly thought-out plan to minimize the number of iterations adds value to the project and increases the value to all stakeholders

Part III:

The Relay Race and Projects

Chapter 8

Mini-projects and Relay Race

> *"Besides the noble art of getting things done, there is the noble art of leaving things undone. The wisdom of life consists in the elimination of non-essentials."* - Lin Yutang

Systematically divide a large project into several easy to manage, quick to deliver sections. These sections are called mini-projects. Mini-projects are the set of activities or processes comprised of repeatable tasks performed by an expert team strung together to create a larger project. This is the transition from one person does all or 'master builder,' to several subject matter experts working in harmony to undertake each section of the project. All mini-projects put together one after another or in parallel in logical sequence shall deliver the intended purpose targeted to be achieved through a large project. Every mini-project has a definite milestone or intermediate objective to be addressed and achieved. Delivery of this milestone represents the progress (% complete) in the larger project.

Most of the time a mini-project can be assigned to an individual work stream that has specific domain expertise in such tasks. This could be an individual subject matter expert, group of experts, external contractors or an internal team consisting of several experts who can execute these projects with total focus and deliver the milestones or objectives successfully.

What is NOT a mini-project?

Any effort which is disconnected from the objectives of the larger project, and any fragmented efforts which are not in line with the overall objectives of the project. Any additional work which has been done over and above the scope of the project is not to be considered as a mini-project.

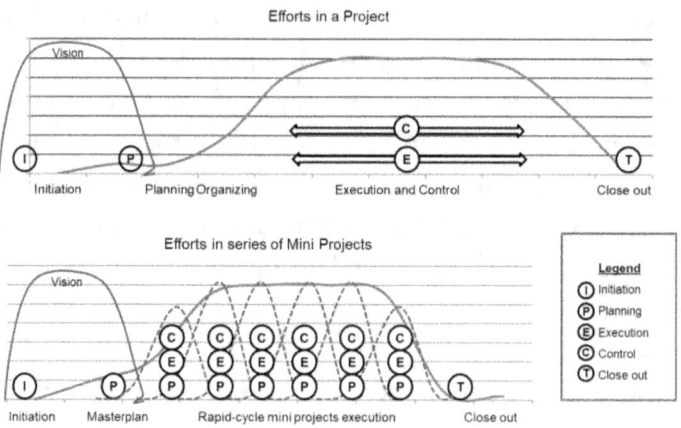

Figure 16: Efforts in large project lifecycle and mini-project lifecycle

Repeatable Processes

Our popular culture idolizes heroism, and we love to romanticize the achievements of those who appear larger-than-life. From Broadway to Bollywood, a lone crusader is capable of saving the world from an alien horde or destruction by the tidal wave, but, surprisingly, in our very real and complex world, there is no such thing as executing a project entirely on one's own. Our organizations tend to be set up in functional departments which allow each discipline to perform its own tasks supported by the experts of related disciplines in other departments, on an ad hoc basis or as part of temporary or virtual teams. Each of these teams contributes their expertise and values in order to create the desired results of a project collectively. For instance, testing or quality control must be performed after software development or the manufacture of a product is put in place to make sure that the intermediate or end product is of appropriately high quality and will consistently meet the intended purpose as per the specified requirements. They have a set of procedures to be followed to verify this. These procedures are repeated for every relevant piece of software developed. The amount of work and the time taken to release each product might vary, depending on the complexity of the product. However, the workflow and set of principles to be followed remain the same for each individual team. In such a scenario, it is prudent to define a repeatable workflow in which this team can process the project. This gives an added advantage of learning from past projects allowing the team to work faster and reduce transition time between projects.

Enable Continuous Improvement

One of the significant failures in the large project process, as practiced in many organizations, is the lack of institutional learning. In the worst case, no benefit at all is gained from the experience from previous projects. In the best case, a lesson learned log is created at the end of each project. Not only is this too late for similar projects which may be running in parallel, but in reality, it is quite rare that these learnings are truly incorporated into the process of improvement, even in future projects. This is evident when the same mistakes recur time and time again across the organization and across multiple projects. Were the learning truly passed on, recurring errors could be prevented and the predictability and success rate of completing projects on time would increase.

In a mini-project environment, governance happens at a more local level, and each of the teams has its own operating perimeter. It becomes simple and straightforward for these teams to define their workflow, execute a specific part of the project, and continually drive increases in efficiency as their experience increases. Project after project, the process gets refined, as the flaws in the workflow can be addressed in-situ and the lessons learned applied immediately in the next task or subsequent project.

Evolution of workflows and checklists are two essential elements of continual improvement in an organization. Workflows define the set of steps to be undertaken in order to accomplish a mini-project goal. A checklist comprises of all of the small details and actions which must be monitored or performed to ensure that each activity in the workflow is done right. In turn, we can deliver the objective to full scope and quality. The checklist can be used to ensure readiness and availability of all the right inputs to a process, and monitor process outputs, as a quality check; all of these drive towards improvement. Any missing element identified during this process can immediately be added to the master checklist to prevent error the very next time the same issue is encountered without waiting for the full project to complete.

Unleash Mastery

Executing mini-projects routinely and repeatedly has the potential to improve the skill set of the individual resource or functional team. As they execute the same repeatable process, time after time, project after project, the ability of the resources to execute efficiently and effectively is enhanced. The important pitfall to avoid is not to breed out creative thinking from the process. The point is to ensure that those activities which should be routine activities are handled as routine. Then, when an unexpected challenge comes along, and you can be sure that it will, the expert has maximum available resources of mind to deal with it, maximizing chances of finding an intelligent and effective solution.

Contrast this with the more conventional approach where tasks are assigned more randomly, and expertise is not achieved. When resources are less familiar with the process and even the mundane may be challenging, is this team really going to have the clear-mindedness required to develop a creative solution?

Finally, repetition helps to improve the mastery of a set of tasks. Over time, the resources develop mastery, and they then become the SMEs in those respective areas allowing the organization as well as the individual to grow and benefit.

Standardized, Consistent Processes

One of the primary causes of a project taking longer than expected is that a project is always unique in some ways and those new aspects need to be tackled for the first time. This is true when looking at the project as a whole; however, at a more granular level, when dividing the project into its constituent parts and allocating those tasks to the SMEs and teams performing the work, many activities will be found to be routine processes with some variations to align with the broader project's objectives. By operating at the local, more granular level, we can find plenty of opportunities to standardize tasks. Standardization can be facilitated using numerous tools, including training manuals, formal SOPs (Standard Operating Procedures), checklists, workflows or standardized work instructions. This, in turn, enables a higher speed of execution of the project by reducing turnaround time, set up time and transition time.

Project management plays the role of the coach of the relay race team by orchestrating the race from beginning to end, focusing on each process as it is performed and especially by ensuring that the hand-off of the baton, i.e., cooperation between the discrete resources so that the overall process is as smooth as can be. Meanwhile, the mini-projects methodology is enabling each activity to be performed with maximum competency and speed. Some industries have already partially adopted this methodology as routine. In software projects, for example, testing activities performed after the code is written are routinely handled in this way. Still, there is tremendous potential to adopt these practices across all industries and all project phases. Actual increases in savings and improvements in efficiency would vary depending on project complexity.

The Relay Race Metaphor

> *"Successful innovation is not a single breakthrough. It is not a sprint. It is not an event for the solo runner. Successful innovation is a team sport, it's a relay race."* - Nguyen Quyen

Comparing between executing a mini-project and a large project is like comparing between a relay race and a marathon. Each requires a different skillset, toolset, and mindset, yet in both cases, the goal is to reach the finish line in the shortest possible time.

The Marathon

Classically, the marathon is the single longest foot race run by individual athletes. This unique challenge requires long-lasting stamina and conservation of energy. To succeed in the marathon is to conserve energy by setting a fast-enough pace and keeping it up steadily for over 26 miles so that one's energy lasts right up until the end. This needs an unswerving strategy and a steadfast plan to achieve enduring performance. There are projects which tend to be managed this way having a long and detailed but predictable schedule and strategy throughout. A good example might be the construction of a 20-storey apartment building. While the lobby and penthouse may be special, each residential floor is pretty much the same as the one below it. The number of windows, doors, and garbage disposal units to be installed is known precisely right from the beginning of the project, and progress can be measured just by counting. Marathons are performed by individuals, when is the last time you have witnessed a one-man show in projects? This would have not been even relevant for master builders, like Michelangelo who conceive, designed constructed and commissioned Cathedrals as he would have depended upon various teams in order to finish the project.

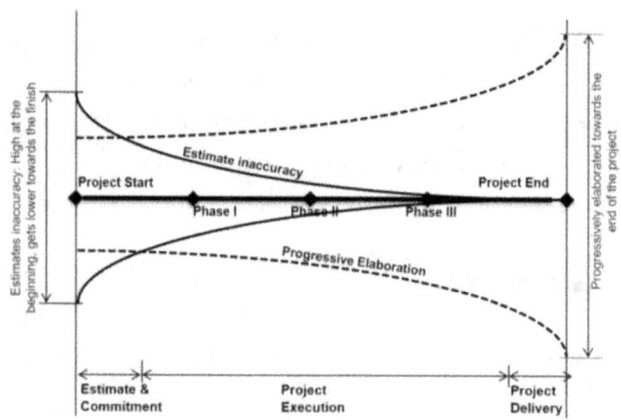

Figure 17: Balancing estimate and progressive elaboration

The Relay Race

A relay race in athletics, on the contrary, is not about conserving one's energy at all. It is about a series of relatively short sprints and bursts of energy by members of a team made up of four runners. Here, the differentiator is the speed of the individual runners and the coordination between them as they pass the baton from one runner to the next. The relay race is about specialization and interface. Projects in many senses are like a relay race, executed by various people from beginning to end. When executing a project like a relay race, we methodically divide the project into its constituent parts as mini-projects, and assign each part to a different functional team. Speed and coordination remain the prominent factors of success.

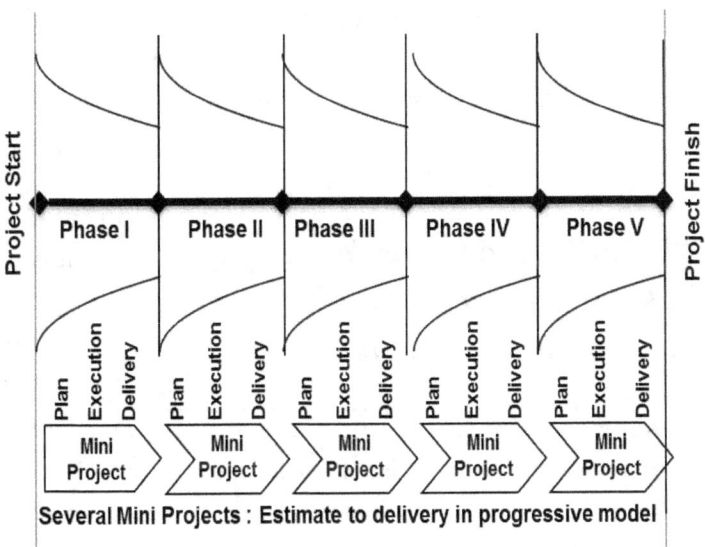

Figure 18: Mini-projects Lifecycles

Projects have evolved as complicated, integrated endeavors wherein multiple domain experts are engaged at every step of the lifecycle. These groups are interdependent, and comprehensive knowledge transfer between them at every transition point is vital. However, each discipline is distinctive, and the very character of the work performed by each is unique to that field. For example, in planning a clinical study, the physicians work in a totally different environment than do the lab technicians, who in turn have a unique working environment compared to the statisticians. To treat them as if they were all minor variations on the same theme would be a mistake and lead to the creation of a bad project plan. We may be able to rely on similar planning techniques and tools to build each section of the overall project model, but we must always bear in mind the distinctive character of each group. This marathon-like approach describes those deterministic planning models that fail to address this problem at the time that the initial project plan is prepared and commitments to ourselves, management and customers are made.

> *In reality, today's project is more like a relay race, where multiple teams participate in the race.*

Even in an athletic relay race, as stated by Jon Drummond (the 2012 Olympics relay coach for the United States); there are specialists for each of the legs. The first leg requires the most explosive runner; the second, a good long-distance runner; the third, a turn specialist; finally, the fourth, the fastest of the four (Kesterson). The speed of all four runners as individual athletes as well as the team at exchange zones while passing on the baton determines

The Relay Race Metaphor

their success. Likewise, as the project progresses, the baton is passed on to various teams, one after another, and there is a need to focus on every section of the project in order to increase the speed of work and achieve the desired goal. The time to complete the overall project is determined by the speed of the individual critical steps of a project.

In a relay race, it only takes one bad transfer of the baton or one slow leg to lose the race, even if the other three racers and hand-offs are technically perfect. Similarly, in projects, all the accumulated delays are passed on downstream, and there is an unreasonably short time limit for the latter-stage work streams to deliver. There is a 'near-death experience' at the delivery point of every project for the project team—particularly for the work streams at the end of the project who invariably need to race against time to meet the project deadline. The team is often required to make very difficult decisions between time and quality, and all too often it is quality that takes a backseat in the time-sensitive project delivery expectations and commitments! It is crucial to remember that the only justification for improvement in local optima is to improve global optima, not for its own sake. If runner number three beats every other runner on the field, but this speed comes at the expense of the quality of the handoff of the baton to the next runner, maximizing local optima would have come at the *expense* of the global optima. Like a relay race, every leg of the project must have the same pressure to deliver each task individually on time but not at the cost of quality. Each team must be focused on the successful execution of their own objectives to full scope and quality in order to "win the race" and truly accomplish a successful project as a whole.

Communication Crusade

Planning a project as a marathon results in the integration of its stakeholders for the entire width and depth of the project lifespan. As a result, there is a tendency to keep everyone involved in status updates, decision making and resolution of issues.

> *The problem in today's projects is often not lack of communication, but overwhelming communication.*

Thanks to the digital revolution, people get hundreds of e-mails every day, which may be related to any aspect of the entire project. In reality, only a fraction of those notifications would be relevant to anyone activity leader's work, and even fewer would actually require a response. As in a marathon, people are expected to keep the entire team posted in the proceedings. People are far too busy and distracted monitoring, reading, and, when necessary, responding to e-mails, leaving less time for productive work; not reading e-mails is considered an indicator of non-involvement.

The overwhelming meetings is another huge distraction and time waster keeping people from getting their tasks completed in a timely fashion. If a meeting needs to be held at all, it should have a well-defined purpose (agenda) with a predetermined time allowed to resolve the issues at hand

and only involve those who are needed for the discussion. Those that need to know the outcome can be updated quickly rather than waste valuable time only to show that they are indispensable to the organization.

Enhanced Level of Performance in a Relay Race

A relay race is one that requires four athletes to participate in place of one, but the result is the increased speed which is not possible by an individual runner even if that runner is Usain Bolt. It is a wonder that no one ever complains about the use of excess resources in a relay race. In fact, all four runners are capable of running the entire distance, yet they choose to come together in order to do something special. They demonstrate teamwork. Relay races illustrate the power of synergy on the tracks. While an individual sportsperson is capable of running the entire race, and they do also participate in individual events, they choose to be a part of a team in order to achieve something which is not possible with the capabilities of one individual. The difference between individual records in a 1500-meter race and a 4 x 400 relay race which is a hundred meters longer than the individual race is impressive enough for us to consider this as a metaphor. Teamwork breaks through the limitations of individual achievement; the only prerequisite is the willingness of passing on the baton. Here is the all-time high achieved by the best athletes in the world.

4 x 400 meters relay race all-time high (Wikipedia)

Rank	Time	Team	Nation	Date	Place
1	02:54.3	Andrew Valmon, Quincy Watts, Butch Reynolds, Michael Johnson	United States	22 Aug'93	Stuttgart
2	02:55.4	LaShawn Merritt, Angelo Taylor, David Neville, Jeremy Wariner	United States	23 Aug'08	Beijing
3	02:55.6	LaShawn Merritt, Angelo Taylor, Darold Williamson, Jeremy Wariner	United States	2 Sep'07	Osaka

The all-time best in a 1 x 1500 meters race is as below

Rank	Result	Athlete	Nation	Date	Location
1	03:26.0	Hicham El Guerrouj	Morocco	14 Jul'98	Rome
2	03:26.3	Bernard Lagat	Kenya	24 Aug'01	Brussels
3	03:26.7	Asbel Kiprop	Kenya	17 Jul'15	Monaco

These results are truly dramatic with a team in the 1,600-meter relay cutting a whopping 31.7 seconds off the time an individual athlete took to run a 1500-meter race, running 100 meters less! The teamwork indeed raises the bar of the performance of the total project as well as the performance of the individual participant.

Real Life Project's Relay Race

Projects too have multiple phases which are carried out in series and in parallel. The relay race does not have parallel tracks the way that projects do and it is rare that projects consist of steps that can only be done serially, one after another from start to finish. There are bound to be parallel phases that ultimately converge with the main path or finish line of a project. These are known as "integration points."

> *The crux here is to find out the core flow and apply the mini-project's methodology and execute as a relay race.*

The core flow is often represented as a critical path, which determines the length and, hence, the completion date of the project. Since it is the critical path that represents project progress, this path needs to be converted into mini-projects first. It is entirely possible that once the mini-project planning is done for the activities on the critical path, we may even find that with the improved timing, the chain of activities previously identified as the critical path no longer is! Thus, we need to work in iterations, planning the remaining activities using mini-project thinking.

Remember that some of the side tracks are "close to criticality" making them equally important as the core track in that if they are delayed by even a small amount, they may themselves become the critical path. So, they also need to be managed as a mini-project. Some of the other side tracks could be service units which might have more slack. These are best dealt with as deliverables to be tracked using a checklist at the integration point. These prerequisites are best dealt with during routine phase review, ascertaining the readiness to start the subsequent mini-projects. Here too, there is no single rule that fits all. The objective is to accelerate the project. Hence the mini-project methodology should be applied to all those tracks be it critical, close to critical or non-critical (aka., about to become critical if not attended to).

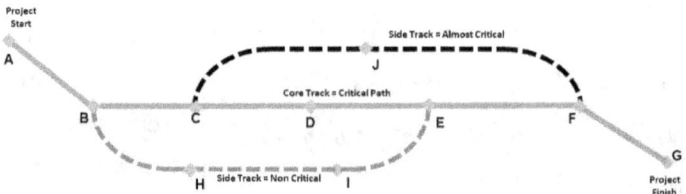

Figure 19: Core flow in projects

In the above diagram, if the critical path is ABCDEFG, then each segment in this path needs to be considered as a candidate to be converted to a mini-project if at all possible. In parallel, there are two side tracks, CJF and BHIE. In this illustration, CJF is not on the critical path. However, because it is close to criticality, it needs to be managed just as carefully as if it were, assigning specialized domain experts to engage in completing these tasks. Thus, CJ and JF also need to be considered as mini-projects and to be handled accordingly.

Chapter 10

How to Create Mini-Projects from A Larger Ones

> *"The responsibility of leadership is not to come up with all the great ideas, but to create an environment in which great ideas can happen."*
> *- Simon Sinek*

Having a compelling vision is an essential first step in any creative process, and this is as true for projects as for any other initiative. The purpose needs to be defined clearly and distinctly because it is this purpose that serves as our compass and, in turn, directs all efforts towards overall success. Without a clearly elucidated vision, the use of mini-projects would only lead to fragmented efforts. Hence the real first step in creating mini-projects from a larger one is to determine the purpose of the larger project unambiguously.

Create a compelling vision

The purpose is something that the customer wants from the product, service, or result that the project aims to deliver. As Harvard professor Theodore Levitt says,

> *"People don't want to buy a quarter-inch drill; they want a quarter-inch hole!" (martin, 2009)*

People buy products and services to fulfill a 'job to be done' or to achieve a goal. Similarly, every project is initiated with an ultimate purpose in mind.

The purpose is determined by the benefit to the customer, or in other words the value that is created for the customer. Simply put it is to answer the question 'what does the customer want?"

Time, cost and scope are not the purposes, but only project parameters and they can be determined after identifying and clearly characterizing the need to be met by the product or service developed. These project parameters can later be used to help in measuring the health of the project while working to complete the project.

A primary reason for new product failure in the market space stems from incorrect assumptions being made about the unmet needs of the customer. The purpose of the project needs to be defined right up front and should be done by or together with the marketing team that is in close touch with the needs of the customer. The marketing team employs their own market research tools in an attempt to fully understand the true unmet needs and the value of the product or service to the customer. Failure to pay sufficient attention to understanding and defining the purpose of a project at the initial stage, in the best case will lead to significant course correction, rework further downstream and change of scope, and in the worst case to total project failure!

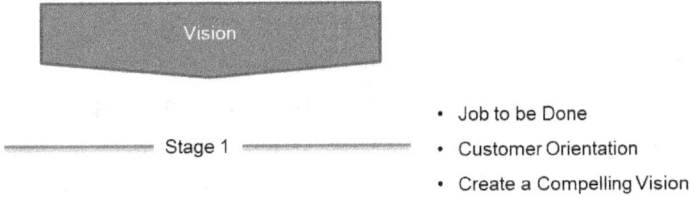

Figure 20: Workflow of Projects @ Relay Race

Think about the project like a ship at sea. If the captain knows the destination and the route and clearly communicates this to all on board, the crew will make all efforts to sail the ship in the same and right direction. Failure to clearly define the destination and route will result in each crew member deciding for himself where he thinks the ship needs to sail, apparently not a good recipe for a successful voyage.

Masterplan - The Blueprint

Once the purpose is made plain to all the next step is to create a blueprint for the achievement of this objective.

This consists of a high-level plan which represents the various phases which the project must complete in order to achieve the intended purpose. A master plan is "a high-level, directionally correct" plan that is to be executed in order to achieve the project's objectives

Every project has a core flow—the sequential set of phases (a.k.a., mini-projects) that are to be performed one after another, to accomplish the final objective. Defining the core flow is the first step in preparing a project master plan. A master plan is an approximately right model of the project. At this stage, the accuracy of estimates is not the target. It is a reflection of the core flow, and its progress represents the overall progress of the project. This blueprint will include interim objectives to be achieved along the way to attaining the larger purpose. High-level cost and time estimates can be derived from this model, but only to get a rough idea of the feasibility and viability of the project, allowing some margin of error and a cushion for cost overruns.

A project, and especially a project which has a high degree of uncertainty, need not be estimated accurately at the beginning.

The rule to be applied is 'it is better to be approximately right than exactly wrong.'

Planning is not for planning's sake, but to create a model that will guide the project team in the execution of the project. Hence, the purpose of the planning is not to delay or complicate execution, but to enable it.

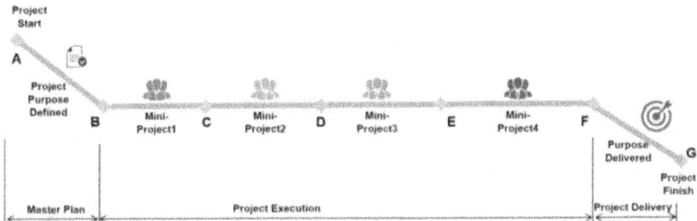

Figure 21: Systematically convert large projects into mini-projects

Split into Mini-Projects

This master plan logically divides the larger project into several phases which we refer to as mini-projects. While breaking the project down into several phases, some of the following ideas can be useful in breaking the larger project down into mini-projects logically:

• The project can be logically divided into phases according to discipline: An example is of analysis, development, test, and release in a typical software development project.
• Critical decision points such as go/no-go are needed
• Delivery of a significant interim objective such as the completion of the proof of concept.
• Transition point from one work stream to another, such as from the research team to the production team or third-party contractor

- Transfer of knowledge from one individual or work stream to another, such as outsourcing part of the project to an external vendor/partner.

As per the first example, above, one logical division into mini-projects can be according to the phases of the project. This can be done regardless of the magnitude and nature of the project. For example, a software development project may logically be divided into the following phases. This is an example of a project of a relatively short duration of a few months or up to a year.

- Requirement Gathering & Analysis
- BRD - Business Requirement Design
- SRS - System Requirement Specification
- Design
- Functional Design - Functional Specification Document
- Technical Design - Technical Specification Document"
- Implementation or Coding
- Build/Coding - Involves Unit Testing
- Testing
- SIT - System Integration Testing
- UAT - User Acceptance Testing
- Deployment
- Production Release Preparation
- Go-Live
- Maintenance
- Transition
- Sustainment

How to Create Mini-Projects from A Larger Ones

An Engineering, Procurement and Construction project (EPC project) can be divided into the following phases; this is an example of a medium duration project which spans out for a few years.

- ☐ Conceptualization
- ☐ Initial Specification
- ☐ Front End Engineering Design
- ☐ Detailed Engineering
- ☐ Procurement
- ☐ Construction
- ☐ Installation
- ☐ Commissioning
- ☐ Support

Pharmaceutical product development is an example of a long-duration project which may span out over ten years or more. A pharmaceutical product development research project can be divided majorly into three segments, called Discovery, Development, and Delivery. This can be further divided into the following phases

- ☐ Drug discovery
- ☐ Target discovery and drug design
- ☐ Preclinical safety and efficacy
- ☐ Proof of Concept and Phase I
- ☐ Drug development
- ☐ Clinical development (Phases II and III)
- ☐ Tech Transfer and Production
- ☐ File NDA - Registration
- ☐ Delivery
- ☐ Marketing Authorisation

- ☐ Launch of the product
- ☐ Life-cycle program
- ☐ Phase IV clinical trials to monitor adverse effects
- ☐ Add new indications
- ☐ Improve existing formulations of the drug

While these are primary phases of the Lifecycle, each work stream has domain experts or subgroups based on the phase or discipline in which they operate. These subgroups have different skillsets and toolsets to perform their respective part effectively. For instance, an oversimplified version of the subgroups in a pharmaceutical development project team is depicted below:

Pharmaceutical Research and Development:
Early Stage Development, Preformulation
Lab Development,
Pilot Scale – (Transfer to Commercial Production Facility)
Scale Up and Process Validation
Production:
Lab-scale,
Pilot Plant Scale-up, Validation
Product Launch
Commercial Production.

Preclinical and Clinical Development:
New drug discovery
Toxicology and preclinical
Phase I
Phase II
Phase III
Post-marketing – Phase IV,

How to Create Mini-Projects from A Larger Ones

Packaging:
Packaging and Label Development,
Production,
Global Packaging management,
Lifecycle management

Regularly Affairs:
Submission of IND
End of Phase II Meeting
First Submission of the complete dossier
Subsequent Global Submissions
Lifecycle Management

Quality:
Quality is ubiquitous in pharmaceutical projects, while each of the phases requires its own specialists to ensure product excellence

Each of these subgroups operates in their respective mini-projects, which collectively represent the entire lifecycle of the project.

Every mini-project can have 'input – activities – output' model. The activities are to be outlined at a higher level at the time of making the initial masterplan but need more granular planning before the initiation of the mini-project along with the progress review.

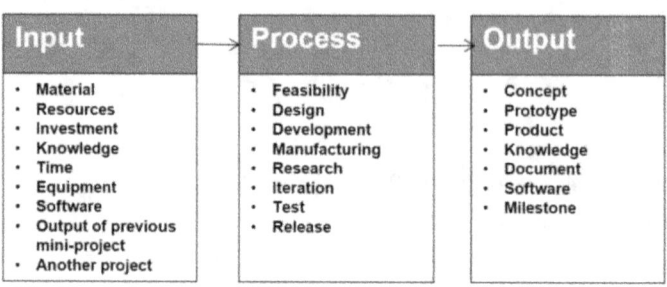

Figure 22: Input – Process – Output model

There is no rule of thumb by which to calculate a "right" number of mini-projects while splitting a large project. This will depend on all of the factors that were described above, and especially on which team is involved and clearly defining what is to be achieved.

> *A mini-project shall conclude with a significant and well-defined deliverable.*

Thus, each critical or core-flow mini-project represents project progress, and successful completion to full scope reflects the quality of the development of the project. The number of mini-projects will also be determined by the amount of control needed in the overall process and the frequency of decision-making needed

Assign Owners and Exit Criteria

Each mini-project needs to be assigned to a single "owner" who will be accountable for the success or failure of that mini-project. The most straightforward example of this would be a situation in which an SME is assigned as the owner of a mini-project which he will also execute. In this case, he is both responsible for performing the work as well as accountable for its success or failure. However, there are less obvious situations, for example, when the resources responsible for the execution of the work are third-party contractors. These contractors are, no doubt, responsible for getting the work done, but we still need to identify an owner within the organization and who will be held accountable for the success or failure of the work performed. An intermediate example of this would be a mini-project assigned to an SME team, for example, an in-house testing laboratory, where any of the numerous interchangeable resources may be assigned to do the work. An owner needs to be assigned and will be the single person who is accountable for the delivery of the milestone. This person may be from the testing laboratory itself, perhaps a team leader, or maybe from the department that developed the prototype to be tested, or possibly a project manager, depending on the structure and culture of the organization. Again, the captain of a ship is a good example of ownership. While the captain has crew members, who are responsible for multiple aspects, the captain holds the accountability for the safe delivery of the ship, its passengers, cargo and crew to its final port of call.

The mini-project is complete when documented evidence that the predefined exit criteria are satisfied. Failure to meet this standard would mean that the downstream mini-project owners would have to adjust for any scope irregularities. This is presented in a negative way since most such anomalies are negative and would cause additional work for the downstream stakeholders.

The Handover Process

In a large project, the seamless transition from one stage to another is vital. There is a handover process between two mini-project owners that enable the collaboration between the two teams responsible for performing the work. The sending team, which has completed their part, hands over to the receiving side, which is responsible for executing the next step. The sending team needs to present all relevant data, project progress, lessons learned, challenges faced and any future risks they have considered, as well as mitigation plans to the receiving side. The receiving unit will review a comprehensive checklist of activities and quality standards to ensure that the deliverable being transferred has been executed in its entirety and that they will be able to continue the project from that point onwards. If there are any pending tasks or outstanding issues, an action plan is agreed upon between the two teams to complete the same. This may allow the handoff to happen conditionally, with no loss of time to the project.

Phase Reviews: Progress Reviews In Between Two Mini-Projects

While the stated purpose of the project is the primary objective of all mini-projects, the suitability to the larger purpose needs to be confirmed at regular intervals in order to ensure that the integrity of the project is still intact.

The reviews between mini-projects are aimed at the following:

- Completeness assessment of the previous mini-project or project
- Handover from one work stream to another
- Pressure test quality of the progress so far
- Check outside-in aspects—external factors that influence the viability of the project.
- Review timeline, and budget to complete the project. Authorize any irregularities in the schedule or budget that could not be made up for by the project team. This may include additional resources, time or budget.
- Review feasibility of project – can still be done to scope, time and budget and confirm readiness to initiate the next phase
- Confirm plan for the next mini-project with a granular schedule based on progressive elaboration.
- Business review of the project 'go/no-go' decision for proceeding to the next steps, if all the above are successful.
- Quality checks and adjustments or take 'go' or 'kill' decisions.

Feasibility Checks: Progress reviews are important to allow the business to reconsider and recalibrate the project from time to time—not of all mini-projects, but those that need to be examined by the leadership sponsoring the projects. This ensures leadership alignment and commitment of further resources. While proceeding with a project, there may be many changes in the marketplace as well as the business environment concerning strategic, operational and tactical elements—a project is not insulated from these events. Traditionally, project teams are focused primarily on the project itself and are less aware of changes in the external environment. As a result, by the time the team realizes that the product is no longer viable for the market, it is already too late. Even this outcome is better than trying to launch a product into an unaccepting marketplace, but clearly, it would have been better and more economical to have discovered this earlier in the process. This can be avoided by having the proper governance mechanisms in place to ensure regular reconfirmation of the product viability throughout the entire project lifecycle.

Remember, canceling a project early costs a lot less than canceling a project later. Good governance dictates that periodic technical and commercial reviews, using updated checklists and templates, are the key to catching feasibility and viability issues in real time. This way, resources, and investment can be allocated to the highest priority projects while those of lesser value is canceled.

While dropping a project is an extreme example and hopefully will not happen too frequently, this review will help in finer adjustments so as to meet the ultimate purpose of creating the highest value portfolio for the future of the business.

Having a well-considered risk register complete with mitigation plans in place should those risks be realized can contribute to the expedited and seamless implementation of those options should the need arise.

Quality Check: Unlike conventional practices, the mini-project approach provides a built-in means of carrying out a quality check at every milestone, by design. This helps the project team evaluate the progress thus far, and ensure that each deliverable is fully achieved before moving on to the next step. At the end of a progress review, the performance report that covers the project's performance up to the current stage, project metrics, projections, and variance report needs to be shared to ensure that the current status of the project is communicated to the stakeholders.

Haunting Past: Once a mini-project is completed—and prior to moving on to the next one—the interface or handoff reviews act as a release checkpoint. Many times, one realizes that a half-done job allowed to be passed on to the next stages would create problems later on in the project, hence, the objective of the interface review is to look at the mini-project that was just completed and ensure that all target objectives were attained in full. Proceeding to further stages of the project without securing this would lead to time and effort being spent on sorting out ramifications at a later stage, and likely result in disruption of the project. Even small steps that are ignored in the earlier stages of the project become an impediment to complete the project. Some common traps include statutory approvals and procurement of components that might be required at a later stage. If there are any pending activities, the team needs to come to a consensus as to whether they should proceed to the next mini-project or not.

Some tasks are critical and must be completed before proceeding to the next one, while others may not be but still have to be completed in order to ensure the project's quality. Thus, an action plan needs to be agreed upon by the project team and followed through until completion.

If a mini-project is found to be partially or entirely unsuccessful, the options are to complete or even repeat the activity or, when not critical to the next stage, to proceed to the next steps with some concrete actions to be completed by a set date.

The review at the end of the mini-project is an opportunity to:
1.   Confirm the robustness of the progress so far, to ensure there are no pending actions that could come back to haunt us in the future. This can be considered an inside-out view of the tasks completed so far.
2.   Ensure that customers or sponsors are part of the process and remain engaged and committed to the project by make them a part of the decision-making process.

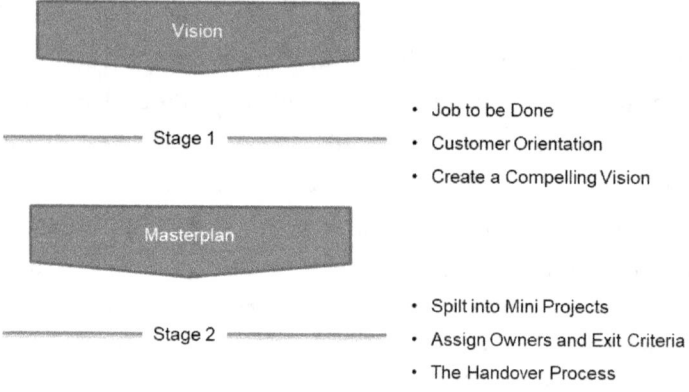

How to Create Mini-Projects from A Larger Ones

Figure 23: Workflow of Projects @ Relay Race

Once a progress review is passed successfully, the path is cleared to move on to the next mini-project for execution, adequately funded and resources committed, including additional resources that might be required by virtue of the nature of the project. The work stream responsible for the mini-project is empowered to execute its portion of the project, take necessary decisions and manage its piece of the project. The team operates as an individual operating unit of the larger project and becomes responsible for on-time, within-budget delivery of the mini-project.

Part IV:

Turbocharge Execution

Executing Mini-Projects

> *"The manned space program is just like a relay race; the landing system is like the runner for the last baton."* - Sui Qisheng

Mini-projects are to be executed in three simple steps: ***"Focus – Finish - Move on,"*** this is analogous to a relay racer's mode of operation. A relay race athlete's mode of operation is unique in three simple ways.

a. When it is time to start, be fully ready - the runner starts accelerating even before the baton is passed, to be up to full speed from the very first measured step

b. Work uninterruptedly at the maximum possible speed when the baton is in hand – the runner does not slow down until after he has handed off the baton; no deceleration while he is still being measured

c. Once the baton is passed, the responsibility is, quite literally out of the runner's hands, and he needs to be ready for the next event in the tournament

Likewise, the approach here is to focus on the mini-project and execute the respective section with no distraction or multitasking in order to drive the larger project with high precision and speed. Each mini-project can be planned meticulously with as much detail as needed. All conclusions drawn during earlier stages and lessons learned from prior activities can be systematically converted into actions and included in the mini-project plan. The accuracy of the mini-project plan, re-estimated just after completing the previous mini-project, is far better than at the starting point of the whole project. If additional resources are required and available, this is the time to allocate them as this is the most essential activity for execution across the entire organization.

Follow the principles: Focus – Finish - Move on. The resources engaged in delivering a mini-project need to "think global, act local." "Think global" means that each person understands the overall strategy of the company and the objectives of the projects to bring it about.

Similarly, each person needs to be aligned with the priorities for these projects and the criticality of the tasks for which he is responsible.

Strong identification with the organization's strategy will improve an employee's engagement and job satisfaction, all leading to happier team members and better performance.

At the same time, no one can be expected to work on all of the projects simultaneously. Act local" means that each member of each team can answer the question, "what is my most critical task today?" So, "act local" refers to focusing on this most critical task and working on nothing else as long as there is work on this task which can be performed. This task must be executed with all due care and speed.

Taken a step further, the team that is responsible for an ongoing, critical mini-project cannot afford to be distracted by any other activity. The rest of the organization is the execution team's defense against external interruption. Don't interrupt or distract people who are working on a critical task.

"Monotasking, not multitasking." This is one of the most important takeaway messages from this chapter. We multitask for many reasons, and always with good intentions. However, the research shows that we are very bad at multitasking and we must avoid it as much as possible. By focusing on one task after another, we finish each task in the shortest time. Only once a task is finished can we move on to the next task. The same goes for the mini-project. After completing the mini-project, the project moves on to the next one through phase review; SMEs move on to the next project in the pipeline and start focusing on their next activity.

Focus

This is a process of "full kitting," readying the current individual mini-project with all its inputs, assumptions and risks, first outlined when the master plan was crafted. As the earlier mini-projects are completed, and the next mini-project looms large, many aspects which could not be seen earlier are revealed, including the manifestation of risks, whose mitigation or rectification can now be planned out in detail in the mini-project plan. For example, when one travels in a car at night, all they see in the light of the headlamps is the next 100 meters. The picture of what lies on the road ahead in the next 100 meters at any given time governs exactly how fast we drive and what steps we take to safely navigate the way forward. The speed of the journey is determined by the conditions encountered in rolling 100-meter segments of the road. In the same way, each subsequent mini-project that is executed will determine the velocity of the project. Hence, the project team focuses on accomplishing the current mini-project with high rigor and speed. The degree of variability and uncertainty decreases and hence can be more accurately planned close to the beginning of each mini-project rather than dealing with nano-planning of unknowns up front, which is sure to be imprecise and inaccurate. At a steady state, while finishing every mini-project and getting to the next, the single mini-project becomes the focal point of the project team as well as the responsible functional team/SME.

As each subsequent mini-project gets close to beginning execution and the project team focuses on it, the accurate detailed plan has to be elaborated. Today's highly academically trained workforce works better when it functions as a self-directed team—hence, the planning for the mini-project is to be done by the execution team, or by a planner, with their consensus. Due to the proximity of the activities, tasks, assumptions, risks, and issues all carry a lower degree of uncertainty than they did earlier in the project or at its start, and a relatively accurate plan can be worked out by the team. The level of detail included in this plan depends on the level of expertise of the execution team balanced against what is required to get an adequate measure of cost and time for that particular mini-project. The higher the level of expertise, the less monitoring of every fine detail will be required and the more autonomy and independence the team will have, A run of the mill construction project can be planned with a much higher level of detail (each window, door, and garbage disposal unit) than a research project with its built-in high levels of uncertainty. Similarly, the research project will need more cushion.

In breakthrough R&D processes dealing with truly innovative cutting-edge technologies, it is likely that multiple experimental iterations are required to deliver a mini-project. At the initial planning stages of the overall project, it would be presumptuous even to guess how many iterations are required and almost any guesstimate would be no better than randomly throwing a dart at a board. However, after having completed early-stage development where some of the uncertainty gets clarified and unknowns get mapped, the level of predictability would be considerably higher at this point in time, and a more reasoned and realistic number of iterations can be estimated for mini-project planning. Resource and cost estimations would be more accurate in such a schedule.

> **Plan for Tasks as well as Idle Time**

A 'watertight schedule' is defined as a schedule that is meticulously planned with highly probable steps, which is impossible to defeat (Robert, 2017). Preparing a watertight schedule, upfront, for an entire project is not possible due to routine variability, various 'known-unknowns' and 'unknown-unknowns.' However, it is possible to get a lot closer for a mini-project under the following circumstances:

a. Steps of the subsequent mini-project are imminent and clear b. Most of the assumptions can be validated and converted into concrete action items

c. There is no ambiguity in the actions and decisions needed in order to perform the activities of next steps

d. Budget and resources for the mini-project are fully committed

For simplicity's sake, we can classify the tasks in a mini-project into two categories—tasks and idle time. Within this, tasks can be further classified into two categories—fixed duration tasks and variable duration tasks. The duration of some, but not all tasks can be shortened by deploying additional resources in executing the tasks. Similarly, some activities can be shortened by deploying additional funds or equipment, or by employing different methods of execution. Other, non-critical activities might actually be lengthened in order to allow the redeployment of resources to more critical activities. Employing these techniques when possible can help in fine-tuning mini-project duration. Careful management of resources can help to control the cost and timing of the overall project. Note that this is true only of variable duration activities. Fixed duration tasks cannot be shortened by deploying additional resources, and require a defined time to accomplish.

An example we are all familiar with is traveling from one place to another. Consider a trip that takes ten hours by road, or four hours by air, including time for airport security and check-in procedures. We can save a lot of travel time if we are willing to pay more money. The duration of the task, traveling from point A to point B, is determined by the time and money available for this particular activity. In real-world projects, this is similar to having multiple dedicated teams, sophisticated equipment, and automated technology to deliver more precise and faster results versus less accurate and more time-consuming manual processes.

The duration of fixed duration tasks cannot be altered by increasing resources or by any other means. An example from the pharma industry is the incubation time for prediction of shelf-life of an ingredient, in-process material or finished product. Consider, a product needs to be held under extreme conditions for six months in special incubators (known as stability chambers) to see if there is a change in product quality in the final package under these conditions. No matter how much money we spend on equipment or people we use, we cannot shorten these 6 months. A more familiar domestic example is the nine months it takes to deliver a baby! Hence, the duration of the non-compressible tasks remains static.

On the other hand, there are idle times that are planned or forced upon us by the nature of certain processes and tasks. 'Planned idle time' occurs when the team waits for a key input or material or a predecessor to complete, and 'forced idle time' is by virtue of the project's nature.

Time Vs. Resources
A watertight schedule will include a series of tasks to be performed sequentially and in parallel as well as some idle time. In an optimum schedule, the variable tasks allow a certain amount of flexibility of resources to shorten or lengthen the overall duration. For instance, for electronic components that have a short obsolescence time but high margins, time to market is far more important than the project cost. Hence, the use of additional resources and investment needed to complete each critical mini-project faster is justified. Projects that are less profitable commodities that must be completed within a limited budget will

at times have to sacrifice time to market, especially if the life-cycle of the product in the market is long.

Project progress is measured in accordance with the advancement of the tasks and idle time consumption. The tasks that determine the overall length of the project are known as "critical" and are used to measure project progress. Completion of these tasks and reaching an interim goal allows us to measure where we stand. However, some tasks do not result in measurable progress after the first few iterations, and it is sometimes difficult to know whether what we have learned from these experiments has led to any project progress at all. During this stage of development, it will be difficult to estimate the remaining duration of the mini-project. However, once a certain threshold is crossed it becomes easier to see the light at the end of the tunnel and estimate time to completion. The last iteration, which results in the effect, represents measurable progress.

Hence, when multiple iterations are needed in order to produce the desired results, it is useful to deploy all available bench-level resources to expedite the progress of the current mini-project. This, in effect, results in an improvement of the overall project. Measurement of progressive time, that created the results versus unprogressive time that does not inch the project forward, is the best way to measure the performance of the mini-project. It is seldom feasible to have estimate accuracy for all mini-project. In a given project, once the prototype is tested successfully and it goes into manufacturing, the uncertainties are fewer. A mini-project with fewer uncertainties can generally be planned with a more detailed schedule. Hence, the granularity of plans can be varied based on the nature of each mini-project as well within a larger project.

Finish

This is where the rubber meets the road, analogous to a sprint of the runner in a relay race upon receiving the baton. While starting a mini-project process, all the prerequisites are lined up in advance, resources are made available, and decisions are taken prior to the mini-project initiation at the previous phase review — hence, at the time of execution when there is no time to waste, no time is wasted. Mini-project execution is purely a well-orchestrated effort to advance the project to the subsequent mini-project without any unplanned idle time. It helps to divide the larger project into several sections, enables focused execution of each resource or work stream through monotasking, and avoids deviation of efforts. It also facilitates the laying out of clear objectives for each section, which is the primary goal for the team until the objective is fully realized. In addition to project tasks, the ecosystem contains many time-wasters, especially meetings and excess communication, which waste the time and sap the energy of the project teams. This can be avoided to some extent through the phase review process. All project-level decisions are worked out up front, so decisions that require the larger team are taken early, during the planning process for the mini-project.

> *This process enables the team to be self-managed requiring minimal intervention from the larger organization, as long as a deviation from the original timeline and budget remain within reasonable pre-authorized limits.*

Since the execution team is adequately empowered to take decisions, large, time-consuming meetings can be avoided. Meetings can be limited in scope to aspects pertaining directly to the particular mini-project and involve only the tasks and coordination between the resources assigned to them. It is critical to provide autonomy for the work stream that processes each mini-project. If planning is sufficiently thorough, many of the inputs or decisions otherwise needed from the larger project team or project sponsors can be converted to conditional 'if-then-else' decisions and authority to navigate the way forward given to the mini-project team. This enables them to focus on execution rather than being caught up in ambiguous situations at the time of execution. Phase reviews need to be well organized, planned rigorously, and managed tightly and decisively to avoid wasting time and to avoid calling redundant meetings during execution. The agenda for these meetings need to include risk management and mitigation plans, empowering the team and streamlining project execution.

Once a particular mini-project is taken up for execution, support from the entire organization must be prioritized, no matter what support is needed by the team. This is because any delay during these critical execution stages will delay the overall project execution timeline. In order to enable velocity, the project teams focus only on these mini-projects one after another, and individual resources need to work on only one task at a given time. It is monotasking that enables speed and not multitasking. It is true that this would depend on the type of the project, and on interconnected activities. However, on the whole, the best way to increase the speed of execution is by monotasking, where the changeover time, diversion of focus and distractions are minimal. The velocity of execution of a mini-project is the single most important factor. It is like a relay race where four runners are running the race, but the overall speed is determined by the one who is holding the baton. Hence, the focus is on the runner who carries the baton for that moment. The speed of the previous runner and the speed of the next runner do not count for that moment in time. Likewise, in a project, the focus is centered on the mini-project that is in progress, and all resources, budget, and capacity subjugated to the current task. Also, this avoids diverting focus towards other activities that may detract from the overall health of the project. The idea is not to have any idle time in the project's execution unless it is necessary by virtue of the nature of the activities or the decision to decelerate the velocity for specific reasons.

Move On

The SME or team can only move on to their next assignment, whether part of the same project or a totally different one, after the closeout of the mini-project. The necessary documentation and knowledge that is to be passed on to the succeeding mini-project have to be prepared to facilitate a complete, seamless transfer. At the master planning stage, the initial estimate of time, cost and resources might have been sufficient. Now that the mini-project is completed, it is a good time to recalibrate the larger project with the actual cost and time taken and estimated to complete the project. For instance, if the project has progressed halfway through, a comparison of the cost and time estimated as part of the master plan and the actual sum of the cost and time taken until this phase will help in assessing whether the project is on track as per the pre-determined objectives.

Like Ford revolutionized the manufacturing industry with progressive assembly, projects also have tremendous potential to harness the efficiency of local optima.

> *Specialization has become very common across large organizations. Employing the progressive assembly concept to the project domain can help to maximize the productivity of SMEs that handle subsets of the project.*

This can be facilitated by "full-kitting," ensuring that everything needed is lined up in advance so that every mini-project can be delivered faster and more efficiently. This is particularly beneficial for programs that consist of many projects done by multiple expert groups for each functional segment of the project. Focusing on improving the efficiency of each section, improving performance based local optima, employed correctly can help in enhancing overall project performance.

Executing Mini-Projects

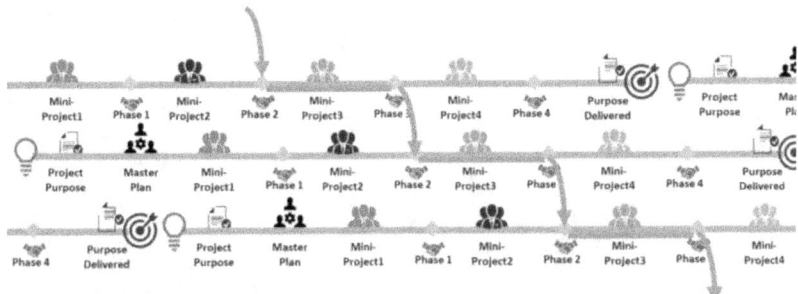

Figure 24: Monotasking for a single work stream in a multi-project ecosystem

When a larger project is divided into several mini-projects, the organization maintains greater control over intermediate deliveries, clear accountability, more accurate schedules, improved focus, and increased velocity. Also, intermediate deliveries improve morale by celebrating small victories and milestone achievements for the individual work streams and enhance the seamless transfer of projects from one segment to another until the finish.

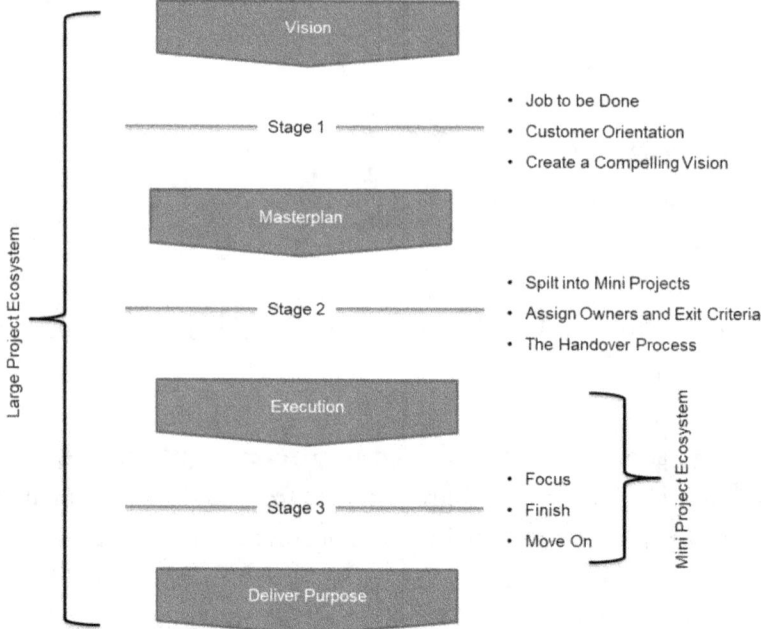

Figure 25: Workflow of Projects @ Relay Race

To summarize, a cognitive project is a creative endeavor that converts ideas into useful products, services or results. The vision or objective is the purpose it needs to fulfill, and all steps are designed to contribute to achieving this goal. Projects must focus on the purpose more than anything else. Progressively unfolding projects must be progressively planned. Being prepared for something that was not foreseen through proper risk mitigation plans is required for reaching the objective on time and on budget. There is always the possibility of undertaking course corrections if a project is not aligned with predefined objectives or to catch up with the technology and to be relevant in the market space. Mini-projects count on the execution team's ability to deliver the project as it is progressively elaborated. It allows for scope change where needed, to achieve the intended purpose. It enables fast and nimble response and breaking the inertia in order to meet the objective of the project. This model values flexibility in project execution as long as the project achieves the desired objective it is intended to deliver.

Part V:

What's in it for Me?

Chapter 12

Benefits

> *"Our current business operating system—which is built around external, carrot-and-stick motivators—doesn't work and often does harm. We need an upgrade. This new approach has three essential elements: 1. Autonomy — the desire to direct our own lives. 2. Mastery — the urge to get better and better at something that matters. 3. Purpose — the yearning to do what we do in the service of something larger than ourselves." Daniel Pink*

Easy to Manage, Fast to Deliver

By their very definition, mini-projects are smaller in size than full projects. In addition, it is easier to assign accountability and ownership. As a result, the management is less cumbersome as compared to the entire large project. In fact, some mini-projects will need very little supervision at all, as they can be managed skillfully by the individual domain experts. Micro managing this expert is often counter-productive resulting in extending the time to completion. It is often better to work with them to agree on a challenging target completion date and then support them in attaining that target.

> *People value freedom, and when that autonomy and trust is given to them, they can be relied upon to expend their utmost efforts in order to meet the targets.*

The challenge and excitement of meeting an aggressive timeline create urgency and an adrenaline rush. Furthermore, as each task is achieved and we can tick another box, dopamine is released in the brain giving a feeling of well-being. Hence, with high achieving self-motivated teams, mini-projects need less governance and are easier to manage.

If you doubt the ability of self-managed systems to succeed, have a look at Wikipedia. This online encyclopedia seems to have sprung up overnight and covers so many topics that it seems infinite. Now, consider that the entire enterprise was created with minimal funding and almost no project management. This crowd-sourced reference tool could be seen as a collection of mini-projects, created one entry at a time to achieve personal self-realization by the authors and editors, with no external motivation save, perhaps, for the respect of their peers.

Flexible – Yet Productive

Mini-projects offer flexibility for the SMEs to work out their own modus operandi, as long as they are in line with the overall mission and technical or regulatory requirements of the larger project. The teams can evolve their own rules of engagement, conducive to their work styles, which are often stricter and more productive than externally imposed rules. While flexibility is available, it also enables peak productivity as people are fully engaged in delivering their own commitments. Not force but the sheer will of passion can drive people to go the extra mile whenever needed in order to accomplish great things on time or even ahead of schedule.

Agile and Nimble

Taking course corrections to realign with the objective of the project is a part of the methodology, especially through the phase review process. Moreover, in mini-projects, decisions can be decentralized, so the teams which are responsible for execution are empowered and authorized to make their own decisions. This creates tremendous agility and enables the team with the flexibility and dexterity needed to navigate the intricacies of the mini-project. Teams find their own solutions to challenges and act in order to deliver their mini-projects faster with uncompromising quality when confronted with challenges, surprises, and Murphy coming to dinner.

The Power of Focus

The sun is the main source of energy powering our planet. The energy of the sun is harnessed by plants to create sugar from carbon dioxide and water. Yet the powerful rays of the sun, filtered through the Earth's atmosphere, can be quite gentle, caressing our skin with warmth on a late Autumn's Day. Now, take a small toy magnifying glass, as every one of us has done as a child, probably more than once. Hold the lens in the right direction and angle to the sun and just the right distance from a dry leaf, or a piece of paper and the focus gives the power to generate fire. In many countries in the world, solar panels collect the vast energy of the sun to heat the water for our showers, light up our roads at night and generate electricity for the power grids that supply our cities.

The power of focus is just as great in project management. Focusing only on the right tasks, one by one, with no distraction of e-mails, meetings, or other activities for the same or other projects enables lightning speed project completion. With the clarity of ownership, roles, and deliverables, each of the work streams of the project maintain laser-sharp focus in order to deliver their part of the project successfully.

> *A project team that is focused on the vision of the project and performance of project activities multiplies its powers of execution tremendously.*

There can be only one task that needs to be performed by an SME or work stream at any point in time, the most critical task. Monotasking is built into mini-projects by design. When is it ok to spice things up a bit and do some work on another activity? Simple! As soon as there is nothing else that can be done on priority activity number one! Focus, finish, and then feel free to move on to something different. What task is that? The next most critical, of course!

Sportive and Supportive

Organizations tend to develop silos. Working in this type of isolation from the rest of the organization is fraught with problems from infighting and turf wars to sanctifying local optima over global optima and the grand objective of the large project. Mini-projects connect people to their domain expertise as well as to the larger mission of the overall project. Here sportsmanship plays a vital role. It is ok, even commendable to take a step back, review what we have learned from our successes and especially from our failures, and celebrate. When we see the big picture and ultimate success of the project, we can also sincerely and wholeheartedly recognize and celebrate the successes of others as well as our own. The relay race model pre-empts conflicting interests between cross-functional teams and also reinforces the collective triumph of delivering a larger project together as a team.

Empower the Individual Work Stream/SME

When the people who execute a mini-project are empowered to make important project decisions, take ownership, and create a sense of belonging and identification with the project and its goals it becomes easy for them to produce the results and services needed from their own competence, knowledge, and expertise.

Decentralization, carefully constructed by aligning with the overall purpose of the project, empowers the SMEs and teams to be fully engaged in creating value from their respective mini-projects.

Self-managed teams – the center of excellence

It is just human nature to want autonomy and desire to control our own destiny. When we teach and empower teams to manage themselves, they can responsibly achieve the autonomy and self-realization they crave. In turn, the teams are enabled and empowered to act with competence, decisiveness, and authority. Over time, the team gains more experience and knowledge and becomes a true center of excellence in creating value. Autonomy facilitates the development of mastery allowing the team to develop the skills needed to deliver results and get them right the first time. In this righteous cycle, focus on certain types of tasks builds and enhances expertise, creating trust and enabling autonomy. Tasks are completed faster creating even more reason to give similar tasks to the same team in the future, further strengthening experience, expertise, trust, and autonomy, and the righteous cycle continues. In this way we create, and harness mastery evolved over time by the respective teams to expedite the delivery and enhance the quality of subsequent projects one after another.

Independent and Interdependent at The Same Time

Mini-projects are assigned to workstreams or domain experts, and these individuals or teams have the autonomy

Benefits

to drive their part of the program. When a larger project relies upon the completion of numerous interdependent mini-projects to achieve overall success, everyone gets the appreciation he or she deserves for his or her contributions in reaching this success.

Project teams are interdependent in multiple ways and especially with respect to each other's areas of expertise. The use of mini-projects reinforces this interdependency while seamlessly integrating SMEs and workstreams to create synergy.

> *The mini-project doesn't create competition between SMEs, but rather creates a collaborative platform and common ground where they can come together, share their expertise and knowledge, and watch as the project progresses.*

As ownership of each mini-project is well defined, we minimize conflict and blame between the workstreams. Phase reviews facilitate the completeness check to ensure that there is no omission passed on from the upstream teams to their downstream colleagues. Everyone operates in his or her own area of expertise and the contribution from all other teams is highly regarded at the end of every mini-project. This is indeed the most collaborative way of executing projects with multiple stakeholders

Reduction in Noise at Every Stage of The Project

'Noise' in the project ecosystem is unavoidable and can come from a number of directions. The phone rings, the inbox fills up, the boss steps into your office for a chat about employee evaluations or the great round of golf he had over the weekend. Some of these are very important, and some less so, but when you are engaged in a critical project task, every minute delayed is a minute lost. Learning to block out that external noise and focus on what is really urgent, as we have discussed at length, is a key success factor. Once you have established that your time is dedicated to completing your task, you will be surprised to see how well the organization accepts and adapts to this. Mini-projects facilitate focused communication within and across teams involved in the task at hand and can be of help to us in avoiding the overwhelming communication overload common in large organizations.

Another kind of noise comes from the task at hand. When a team is faced with a new challenge there will always be unexpected issues to overcome even if the novelty is relatively small. Consider something as simple as filling your gas tank, a completely routine task that we all perform frequently. You think nothing of pulling up to the gas pump, opening the gas cap, inserting the nozzle and in no time you are on your way with a full tank of gas. Now go and do the same thing in a rental car of a model you have never driven before in a foreign country. Which side is the gas tank opening on? Is there a release lever to open the cover panel and where is that "hidden"? Which of the three different types of gasoline goes in this car (or was it diesel?!) Why is my credit card not working? Where do I go to pay? What is normally a brief pit stop, in and out, suddenly takes double or triple the usual time and increases levels of aggravation far beyond that. However, the next time that I need a fill-up, at least some of these issues are already solved. I know which side of the pump to pull up on and how to pop the panel. I know to expect that my credit card won't work, and begin looking for the cashier as soon as I pull into the station. Experience is a great teacher!

The same thing is true during a project and any task encountered for the first time. There will be unexpected pitfalls and uncertainty. However, by assigning the same type of task to the same dedicated team each and every time, they will learn the differences between a Toyota and a Suzuki, (hint, no matter what car you are in, the gas pump attendant always knows exactly where the gas panel release is hidden!) The team will know the types of issues to anticipate even if the exact variation has never been encountered before (a known-unknown is much easier to deal with than an unknown-unknown!) When a team executes a task for the first time, it has more noise to deal with, but while repeatedly performing the same or similar tasks, the learning curve kicks in. The errors, common pitfalls, dependency issues, risks, idle time, all become apparent and can be handled effectively before they hamper progress. The workaround options and plan B's can be worked out in advance in order to minimize the noise.

Chapter 13

Underlying Principles

Modern project management had originated, as we've seen, with an interest in scheduling and cost control techniques but then developed as a means of coordination. (Morris, 2013)

A project, by its nature, is a collaborative process and people play an essential role by sharing the larger vision and co-creating the same through their expertise. High performing organizations are integrators and master the art of uniting people from diverse disciplines and with widely varied and sometimes opposing talents. Successful leaders are skilled at bringing out the best in everyone and to use this to keep ahead of the competition by quickly and creatively converting ideas into successful products.

> *The ability to respond rapidly to a changing marketplace has become a critical success factor enabling companies to respond to the unique challenges most industries face while simultaneously pursuing new opportunities.*

Some of the underlying principles which are very relevant in today's environment of ever-increasing complexity are equally important when creating and executing mini-projects.

☐ Creativity and curiosity of the human mind are the most valuable enablers in a larger project. Voluntary engagement is a key to the success of complex projects (e.g., Wikipedia) and to empower the team.

☐ Decentralize: allow teams to solve their own problems and make their own decisions as much as possible.

☐ No master builder, but multiple domain experts' teamwork is needed in order to succeed in projects.

☐ Strengthen everyday collaboration between teams that can govern themselves. Enhance the seamless transfer of projects from one phase to another until the finish. Improve governance and control by simplifying complex frameworks.

☐ Progressively unfolding projects are to be progressively planned to result in greater control over intermediate deliveries and clear accountability through more accurate mini-project schedules that improve focus and increase velocity.

☐ Initial assumptions can go wrong....... yes, you are reading this right. Projects get influenced by the external environment as well.

☐ Don't sweat the small stuff. In other words, it is the objective that is truly important, not the way you planned to get there. Always keep the true objective foremost in your mind and remember that if you can't get over the wall, you may still be able to reach the desired objective by tunneling under it, or drilling through it.

☐ If failure is inevitable, fail early. Similarly, small errors at the beginning, if left uncorrected, get magnified downstream. It is essential to identify and make course corrections as early as possible.

☐ The speed of each critical step determines the speed of the whole project. Helping a constrained or bottleneck resource to reach their local optima contributes to the project reaching its global optima. Focusing on the activity you need to finish now improves the overall velocity of the project. Focus on and execute the current phase of the project with high precision and speed.

☐ Projects are like a relay race, not a marathon.

New Ways of Working

Following are some of the new rules of engagement you can inculcate to thrive in projects amidst chaos and complexity. In fact, in the newer normal, it is not about controlling chaos but it is about living with chaos and thriving with chaos. All these can be done as low-key affairs in any organization. In the projectized organizations, then this can be propagated to create a new way of working.

CREATE A COMPELLING TAGLINE FOR EVERY PROJECT

While the project charter and other documents are prepared at the beginning of the project, there is nothing like having a compelling tagline that connects the execution team to the vision of the project. This can be prominently displayed everywhere remind people of the purpose of the project. The compelling tagline needs to address the value the project intended to create and connects people's contribution towards achieving this. This can be a defining statement that relates to the customer. This invokes the passion of the people and encourages them towards the purpose the project creates

Numbers are not necessarily inspiring, providing project targets with numbers such as complete this within this time and with the budget may not be able to connect to the people who are executing the projects. Creating a compelling tagline that is connected to the contribution of every individual in adding value to the customer or the organization is a powerful tactic that will connect people towards the purpose of the project.

If a project does not have a compelling purpose, it may not be worth pursuing. Be it creating value to the customer, generating new market space, a next-generation product, building a megastructure, creating new products for the company, several of such intents helps organizations to create a compelling vision.

INVOKE A LEARNING ORGANIZATION RATHER THAN MISTAKE-PROOF CULTURE

A mistake-proof culture limits the learning ability of the organization. Moreover, it does not allow issues to surface out quickly for immediate resolution. People tend to suppress the issues, and the ability of the project teams to implement course corrections early enough may not be feasible. Remember the bullwhip effect. Course corrections made in the early stage are better than later as the impact would be multiplied at later stages. 'Everything needs to be done perfectly' is an expectation that brings in inflexibility, and people are always under pressure to deliver right the first time. Mistakes are bound to happen whether we accept them or not. Rather than making a system that does not have tolerance for errors, make the organization and project teams a learning entity. At least this ensures that people learn from the mistakes in order not to repeat the same in the same project or in subsequent projects. This, over time benefits in increasing the reliability of the project team. This is how a mistake can be reduced, not by punishing.

FOSTER ENTREPRENEURS' CULTURE THAN EMPLOYEE CULTURE

The *new normal* projects need an entrepreneur's mindset instead of the employee mindset. Projects are unique and one-time effort, hence involves a lot of ideation in it. Particularly, for the knowledge era, where the cognitive ability influences project's success. Some organizations call their employees partners, this reinstates the importance of the entrepreneurship of employees in creating value for the project as well as organizations. When the project team member becomes partners in the project in a real sense, their ownership and accountability increase multifold. One who is working on saving his/her job will not be able to create value for the organization. But the one who is with an entrepreneur mindset can create products, services, and results at an unprecedented rate.

TASK-ORIENTED TO GOAL-ORIENTED

Task orientation is the conventional approach toward controlling a project. In effect, there are situations where the tasks are tightly controlled, but the project is not approaching towards the end goal. The *new normal* requires focusing on the goals. A shift from the cause to the effect. Any task which is undertaken, if that creates value for the project and advances the project towards completion, is the true measure of the progress. 'I have done my job' is not going to help the project progress.

A parable that demonstrates this is about two contracts working on a highway. One contractor dug holes alongside a road and another one after sometimes came with his tools and filled it with dirt. While asking, they reported that they are doing their job, but another contractor who is supposed to show up in between both of them is needed to plant saplings in the hole, is not reported for the duty. This might look like a weird example, but in reality, when not focused on goals, but merely on tasks, in projects, we end up in such a situation.

'THINKING' PROJECT TEAMS THAN 'CHASING' PROJECT TEAMS

A chasing project team operates from a background of meeting the targets such as time, cost, and scope. A thinking project team is the one who keeps an eye on the very purpose the project needs to create. A thinking project team is the one who always sees the opportunity to add value to the project and eventually to the customers. It has a greater connection with market needs and user experience. Every task of the project is aligned with the larger mission and in the direction of the true north. When something is not in synchrony with the true north, the thinking culture enables a course correction head-on instead of deviating for a long time and firefighting. This eventually ends up achieving time, cost, and scope yet produces surpassing products, services, or results that will subsequently benefit customers.

FROM PROBLEM ORIENTATION TO SOLUTION ORIENTATION

Sometimes you may observe that the project team is passionate about dwelling on the problems. The critical shift which is needed is to be a part of solutions culture. This means being effectively engaged in finding the solution to the issues that might evolve from time to time and keep the ball rolling towards achieving the desired outcomes. This solution orientation comes from resolving issues, finding facts, and putting progress on the front burner. Problem orientation is characterized by exposing people to be blamed, on the contrary, a solution orientation makes people think 'what' needs to be solved rather than 'whose fault is it.'

CONSTRAINT TO OPPORTUNITIES

This is the transformation of triple constrain to triple opportunities that we have seen earlier. Shifting the focus from Time, Cost and Scope to Velocity, Value and Purpose is a game-changer in the *new normal*. Project teams have immense value to add to the *new normal* ecosystem by creating new products, results or services. When project teams consistently deliver the purpose fast enough, that is the success of the profession. That is the contribution of project management to the business, community, and one's own self.

Chapter 14

Bonus: Hack the Happy Hormones

Project management is often mistakenly perceived to be a highly stressed profession. This error in perception is easily understood. Project managers are often faced with difficult situations and challenges that need to be addressed as part of daily life, particularly in the *new normal*. We are told to 'do more with less.' We need to manage conflicts between stakeholders and are responsible to motivate resources to perform in certain ways without the benefit of direct line management authority. But a project manager can derive happiness despite the complexity of these situations. Happiness is, after all, as much of a science as it is a mindset.

This bonus section attempts to provide techniques to hack the happy hormones, the science of attaining happiness. Happiness is contagious. A happy project manager inspires the project team and enhances value in the lives of the stakeholders he or she encounters within the organization as well as externally.

This section is dedicated to the COVID-19 warriors across project teams. Please feel free to share this bonus section of the book with anyone, the authors view this section as a public service announcement and claim no copyright protection for this section.

Energy drinks, when consumed in moderation, make us feel good. They revitalize the body and mind and improve performance. There are numerous legal and illegal, moral and immoral ways of influencing brain chemistry, from extreme exercise on one end of the spectrum, to the consumption of legal and illegal mind altering substances on the other. Yet there is a kind of energy drink that is available absolutely for free that creates the same level of mental and physical 'high'! and moreover, with no harmful side effects, accessible to all and within your reach. In fact this 'drink' has several positive side effects, and thus far no government has banned it, and never will.

You can imbibe daily and keep yourself fit and happy. The brand name that we use for this energy drink is 'DOSE.' There are four major chemicals in the brain that influence our happiness in DOSE:

Happiness - whose job is it anyway?

Many a time we hear people saying, I would be happier if I could only.... <fill in the blank for yourself.> The blank may be filled in by vacation or vocation, by possessions or wealth, by a new car or a bigger house. People generally believe that happiness is connected with external events or materialistic possessions, but the truth is that the moment that these externals are achieved they again long for the next materialistic or external goal to which they aspire. One more thing they aspire for. This wisdom is not ours and it is not new. King Solomon the wise wrote over 2500 years ago that

Bonus: Hack the Happy Hormones

> *"He who loves money will never be satisfied by money and he who loves abundance with plenty"* (Ecclesiastes; 5:10)

Happiness is an inner feeling of contentment, not to be confused with pleasure and not to be obtained through external or materialistic possessions. The good news is that the capability and potential for happiness can be achieved without any of these. We have witnessed the poorest children in the world running and playing happily, seemingly with no reason to be happy at all. Adults, on the other hand, always seem to be looking for reasons to be happy. Like our younger selves, being happy can be a default mode for us. Happiness can be instilled as a habit. A good habit indeed.

We know that each individual is responsible for his or her own happiness. The following are some of the ways in which people stimulate a happier and healthier life, that cost nothing at all. In fact, they are free to all for the taking if we just know how to extend our hand:

1. Positive affirmations
2. Gratitude
3. Love - strongest positive feeling in the world
4. Doing something one is passionate about
5. Mindfulness
6. Yoga

All these things bring happiness and contentment. While we all know this, at least intellectually, if not always intuitively, sometimes it becomes cumbersome to defeat the darker, internal inclinations that would deceitfully draw us into a deep hole. Is there an alternate way to 'hack happiness?'. Neurochemicals pave the way. There is an easy way in which you can get your daily dose of happy chemicals. Wanna try this? Then let's move on.

Have you got your DOSE of Happy Chemicals today?

DOSE is an abbreviation for:

- Dopamine
- Oxytocin
- Serotonin
- Endorphins

These are the neurochemicals that are naturally secreted in the body and stimulate certain feelings in the brain. Let us look at what are they and then how to obtain them, absolutely for free

Dopamine: this is the 'feel-good hormone,' and stimulates the natural reward system in the brain. It helps you to stay motivated to achieve your goals. When someone appreciates you, how does it feel? Great, doesn't it? Yet we tend to reserve that appreciation only for 'big tasks.

Ken Blanchard in his "One-Minute Manager" explains to 'catch people doing right', dopamine secreting way of getting people motivated, happy, and deliver greater performance.

Break your goal into tiny pieces and celebrate every quick win. The celebration doesn't need to be a jubilee. A coffee, a bar of chocolate, a glass of wine or a scoop of ice cream, make it big. Sometimes just a good word. Take the treat. That's how you hack the chemical. There are numerous ways in which you can celebrate small things. We used to offer pizza parties at the office for every small achievement. While pizza is junk food, dopamine does its job. For foodies, consider the tyrosine that can be found in almonds, bananas, avocados, eggs, velvet beans, fish, and chicken.

Another dopamine hack – keep a written to-do list of activities for the day. Every time you complete an activity, cross it off the list. The mere act of crossing each achievement off the list releases a small burst of dopamine and motivates you to complete the next task.

Allow yourself enough sleep and exercise time. Music, meditation and sunlight are some of the other ways to get this Happy Hormone.

Dopamine increases your passion for achieving something. Be it a KPI, or an assignment, or a degree or a project, it consistently motivates you to achieve. The more you motivate yourself, the more you accomplish.

Oxytocin: Often referred to as "the cuddle hormone," a simple way to keep oxytocin flowing is to give an **appropriate** someone a hug. This improves the levels of trust, intimacy, and is strong in building relationships. This hormone is abundantly produced during breastfeeding and pregnancy.

This is secreted by inter-personal touch. Hugging is one of the ways it can be hacked. Hence, every morning hug your children or spouse, or beloved pet. Hug therapy is becoming more and more popular. Following are some of the ways in which Oxytocin can be stimulated

- Cuddling, kissing, hugging, physical intimacy

- Yoga and meditation
- Listening to music, empathetic listening to people
- Sharing with someone how much you care about them
- Spending time with friends
- Random acts of kindness. When we give, we get!

WARNINGS: 1) If you are reading this at the time of COVID-19, keep in mind all the guidelines of social distancing. 2) Any and all touching must be appropriate and wanted, and generally to be avoided in a working environment.

Oxytocin improves trust and relationships. The side effects of this are that it reduces cardiovascular diseases and improves immunity. Do you want to miss this out?

Serotonin: This is a natural antidepressant and confidence booster. This neurotransmitter is secreted when you feel that you are important. The self-ecstasy level in Maslow's hierarchy.

Reflecting on past achievements and reliving the experience in your mind is a simple way to hack this. Taking pride in what you have done is the simple way to hack this. Some other ways to get Serotonin are,

- Be grateful for what status you have achieved so far and how much more you can accomplish going forward.
- Status within your family, community, or organization may be a potent enabler.
- Some lifestyle adjustments like getting into sunlight, aerobic exercise, staying hydrated

- *Say cheese and go nuts*: Eating L-tryptophan-rich foods from eggs to chicken, cheese, turkey, tuna, nuts, beans, lentils, and leafy vegetables,

While serotonin makes you happy, the side effects are improved learning ability and memory boost, appetite, and digestion.

Endorphins: These are the body's natural pain killers and are secreted in the brain as a response to exercise and pain. Endorphins are a natural defense mechanism in life-endangering situations; however, you need not wait for life-threatening situations. Regular stretching of the body and brisk exercise will help your body release endorphins in a regulated way and amount that helps you live comfortably.

Vigorous exercise for 25 minutes a day will result in the secretion of endorphins. Once you cross the threshold of 25 minutes, you will feel the change and remain motivated throughout the day. Try this out and some more additional aspects as below.

- Laughter is not an alternative to exercise, but it will also augment the secretion of endorphins.
- Some research findings suggest that acupuncture, meditation, and medical-massage release endorphins
- Eating spicy food
- Giving away money for a cause
- One more excuse to eat chocolate
- Group exercise like aerobics, zumba, biking, rowing

The side effect of endorphins is that they help to reduce anxiety. Be happy with endogenic happy chemicals!

Is this not enough to be happy and content?

Try a strong version which is called DOSAGE. Particularly in the COVID lockdown situation where life is at a *new normal,* coping up with the additional pressure needs a stronger dose.

Like DOSE, DOSAGE stands for Dopamine, Oxytocin, Serotonin, *Anandamide, Gratitude,* Endorphins. We have seen what D, O, S, and E are. Here are the remaining A and G

Anandamide: Ananda literally means bliss in Sanskrit. This is known as 'the bliss molecule' and acts on the cannabinoid receptors of the body's endocannabinoid system. Exercise, to a level of 25 minutes releases endorphins (Biles, 2017). There are reports that after 30 minutes of exercise, anandamide levels are increased resulting in "runners high.". If you stop within 25 minutes you should be happy with an endorphin shot alone.

- If you want anandamide you will have to stretch more intensely and go to a level of 'runners high'.
- A cold shower in the morning
- Chocolate contains small amounts of anandamide - *another great excuse to consume chocolate.*
- Some of the other foods in which you can get potentially more anandamide include black truffles, galangal, and maca root.

However, there is no better way than getting this naturally from the secret chambers of your cells through intense exercise.

Gratitude: Gratitude is the second strongest force next to love. This bestows a super feeling and acts as fuel for life.

How do you hack: Every day is a thanksgiving day for us. Wake up with feeling gratitude for the new day. In the Jewish tradition, the first conscious act performed upon waking is to recite "I thankfully acknowledge you, the living and eternal King, for returning my soul within me with compassion; great is your faithfulness." Every day some so many people go to bed and never rise in the morning. So, start with that. Whether you believe in God or some other supreme energy that operates in the world, spend the first five minutes of every day in gratitude. Similarly, before going to bed, give thanks for everything good that happened. If anything happened not as you like, rewind the event in your mind's eye as if it happened as you would have wanted it to happen. Give thanks for everything good that happened during the day from the bottom of your heart.

Have you heard about gratitude rock? I learned this from one of my favorite books "The Secret by Rhonda Byrne". This is yet another simple hack that you might try to inculcate the habit of gratitude.

One common requirement to get all these hormones is doing regular exercise. If you like to sum it in a single line to get DOSAE, do any kind of exercise like Yoga or running, jogging, running for about 30 minutes in a sunny light. Many people find that listening to lively music helps energize the activity and adds food for the soul. If you can, exercise with a partner or in a group, especially with your family and friends for even more benefit and added motivation. This will help to ensure that you get your daily dose of happy hormones and neurostimulators to make your life gratifying and energetic, every given minute.

Some people just seem to be born happy, while others struggle to make themselves happy. Now that the secrets to unlocking happiness are known, decide for yourself what actions you want to take in order to be and remain happy. Go on and hack happiness.

I must thank all my gurus who enlightened me with this concept. I learned this concept first in a corporate training program conducted by Jeroninio Almeida (Jerry - Jerry is a teacher, celebrated inspirational orator, motivational speaker, social entrepreneur, and a highly sought management consultant.) Ever since I knew this, I started searching for additional learning opportunities and numerous online teachers on the internet and elsewhere helped me to get to the bottom of it. However, I did not experience anything until I practiced. The more I practice, the more I get. I wish you too can start practicing in order to get the benefit of the high you can achieve with these natural, endogenic happy chemicals.

May the joy be with you!

Extro

I do not need to be a mentalist to guess that if you're reading this you are probably deeply involved in project management, making you a member of a unique and growing club in the *new normal*. Members of this club will identify with the well-known quote "Being a project manager is as easy as riding a bike, except that the bike is on fire, you are on fire, and you're in Hell."

No, project management is not easy, but it is as interesting and rewarding as it is diverse and challenging. There are new problems to solve in newer normal, and as you solve them and measure real project progress your satisfaction grows, nearing you to the top of Maslow's legendary pyramid. Of course, it helps to be an optimist in the Martin Seligman sense, meaning that you believe that your efforts can have a fundamental positive impact on outcome. You must be able to see the glass half full, but this is not the most fundamental reason. You must know that your only responsibility is to drive your project towards successful completion, and that what you do and how you do it will have a major impact upon that progress and success.

I first met John Robert about six years ago and we immediately discovered a shared passion for project management and the values required to drive projects forward and deliver them successfully. During our years of collaboration, it was clear to me that his charisma and vision would drive him and serve him well as a motivational leader in project management. It is for these reasons that, when John mentioned his "Project Management for the *New Normal*" initiative, I was so keen to work with him on it.

The relay race metaphor is not new in project management circles, but John has further developed it, and provided some fundamental guidelines that can be incorporated into any methodology of project management that you are using. One might think that the four runners in a relay race are fully interchangeable, since it is the aggregate of their running times that determines how fast the race is run overall. Just as this is untrue in a relay race, John demonstrates how project resources are not always fully interchangeable, and using the most suitable expert for each task makes a big difference. Experience creates the expertise, which creates more expertise.

Another important takeaway message is the way resources are used. A common fallacy is that everyone needs to be busy all the time, always running to 100% capacity in order to be efficient. John shows how effectiveness is more important than efficiency and that without some spare resources, projects are bound to be delayed because just when a critical task is to begin, the resource may be occupied by another task, lower priority by definition!

Focus on the bottleneck and bringing it, first to full capacity, and then find ways to increase that capacity further is paramount, even if it appears that some (non-bottleneck) resources are under-utilized. Non-bottleneck resources must always be subservient to bottleneck/critical resources. Never forget when executing a project that the critical resources will often shift as criticality moves from one task or function to another, exactly as happens in a relay race.

Perhaps the most important takeaway, however, is John's total commitment to monotasking. No matter how many times we hear it, how many A-1-B-2-C-3... exercises we perform, the necessity to eradicate multitasking cannot be stressed enough. Focusing on one task, finishing it in the minimum possible time and only then moving on to the next task is critical to timely project execution. This can, and often must apply not only at the individual task owner level, but at the team or even departmental level as well.

There are many tools used in project management, and many methodologies employed. From basic Excel, to sophisticated enterprise PM systems, from Agile to Waterfall and Scrum to Kanban, from six-sigma to PMBOK to CCPM, if you follow the rules of "mini-projects" and implement the basics of mini-projects, your performance will be improved.

In fact, this is one of the great advantages and strengths of mini-projects. Anyone who has tried to implement a new project management system in a large organization knows how difficult, cumbersome, time-consuming and distracting it can be. The principles of mini-projects can be implemented immediately in any organization, without disrupting the existing project management methodologies at all.

Project Management for the Newer Normal

Nothing can make management of complex projects in a multi-project environment easy. I mean, they don't compare it to "herding cats" for nothing, right? However, implementing the fundamentals of mini-projects will simplify the job, and you will be impressed with the results you can achieve by embracing these important values.

If you don't belong to the club, you should! Not because project management is easy. It isn't! But embracing mini-projects will simplify the complexity, and, after all, isn't simplifying complexity the name of the game?

Mike Teiler
Kfar Sava, Israel
Sep 2021

Bibliography

Klein, G. (Sep 2007). **Performing** a Project Premortem. *Harvard Business Review*.

http://corporate.ford.com/innovation/100-years-moving-assembly-line.html. (n.d.).

Institute, P. M. (2018). *10th Global Project Management Survey*. Retrieved from Project Management Institute, Inc.: https://www.pmi.org/learning/thought-leadership/pulse/pulse-of-the-profession-2018

Kesterson, L. (n.d.). *The New York Times*. Retrieved from Four Legs, Four Specialists: http://www.nytimes.com/interactive/2012/07/23/sports/olympics/the-fastest-baton-to-the-finish-line.html?_r=0

Martin, D. (2009). *Secrets of the marketing masters: what the best marketers*. Amacom.

Morris, P. W. (2013). *Reconstructing project management*. Cambridge, MA:: John Wiley.

O'Donoghue, T. &. (1999). *American Economic Review*. American Economic Association.

PMI. (2018). *Pulse of the Profession 2018*.

Robert, J. (2017). *Spiral Staircase Project Management*. Notion Press.

Sharot, T. (2011). *The optimism bias: A tour of the irrationally positive brain*. New York: Pantheon/Random House.

Wikipedia. (n.d.). https://en.wikipedia.org/wiki/2007_World_Championships_in_Athletics.

List of illustration

Figure 1: The Pandemic Paradox
Figure 2: Process Groups in a Project
Figure 3: Efforts needed across the project lifecycle
Figure 4: Snake and Ladder game metaphor in projects
Figure 5.1: Resource allocation in parallel projects
Figure 5.2: Smart resource allocation in parallel projects
Figure 6: Shortest path to completion
Figure 7: Unlocking opportunities
Figure 8: Transforming triple constraints
Figure 9: Levers of the Opportunity Triangle
Figure 10: Project Vision Board
Figure 11: The missing process
Figure 12: Forecast inaccuracy in a project lifecycle
Figure 13: Progressive elaboration in a project lifecycle
Figure 14: Large projects in a multi-project environment
Figure 15: Ford's assembly line concept
Figure 16: Efforts in large project lifecycle and mini-project lifecycle
Figure 17: Balancing estimate and progressive elaboration
Figure 18: Mini-projects Lifecycles
Figure 19: Core flow in projects
Figure 20: Workflow of Projects @ Relay Race
Figure 21: Systematically convert large projects into mini-projects
Figure 22: Input – Process – Output model
Figure 23: Workflow of Projects @ Relay Race
Figure 24: Monotasking for a single work stream in a multi-project ecosystem
Figure 25: Workflow of Projects @ Relay Race

Acknowledgments

Writing a book is easier than I thought and more connecting to the world than I could have ever imagined. None of this would have been possible without the experience I had in the corporate world. I'm eternally grateful to all the organizations I have associated with and the project teams I have worked with in the past two decades. This thought me the nuances of leading a project, be it normal times or *new normal*, or even newer normal. This taught me challenges, realities, risks, opportunities in a real-world project. I truly have no idea if I would have written a book without the challenges which I have faced along with my team in executing projects and constructing PMOs.

Very special gratitude to Mike Teiler whom I approached for editing this book and ended up enriching the contents and thus become a co-author. All that Mike needs is perfection, thanks to his professional OCD, he does not leave a comma or full stop or consistency until it gets corrected. Mike and I worked together, we were able to share the passion for projects and able to continue the partnership through this book as well. Mike, thank you for adding value to this book manuscript.

To my family. To Mary, Sheron, and Thanya: for always being my backbone in the writing part of my career and the other passion, wildlife photography. You are the people I could turn to during challenging times. So thankful to have you in my life.

About Authors

John Robert

John Robert is a project leadership enthusiast with two decades of experience in projects, engineering, and operations. He has significant exposure in large-scale infrastructure projects and complex research program management. John is an engineer and MBA by education. He has 360degree exposure as a sponsor, consultant, project manager, leader, and contractor, from simple brick and mortar projects to ERP implementation to complex research and development programs.

While many of the projects he led were successful; he also had his share of failures.

He considers his experience of challenging projects are more valuable, the projects that have not met the time, cost, and scope targets. Many of them failed despite adopting the best practices of project management. His quest is in search of a solution to this; you will find this reflected in his writings. He uses metaphors that simplify the concepts to make the ideas simple, including his first book Spiral Staircase Project Management.

More about his products and passion on www.mjohnrobert.com. He can be contacted through email (johnrobert99@gmail.com) or LinkedIn (https://www.linkedin.com/in/johnrobertmanuel)

Mike Teiler

Mike Teiler was born in the US where he lived with his parents and two younger brothers through high school graduation. After spending a gap year (or two) in Israel, Mike enrolled at the Hebrew University of Jerusalem, earning a Bachelor of Pharmacy degree.

Following graduation, he joined the R&D department of the second-largest pharma company in Israel at the time, only to be acquired by Teva Pharmaceuticals less than a year later where he served in ever more senior R&D and Portfolio Management roles until leaving after 24 years as VP R&D for Teva's International Group. This was followed by a six-year tenure at Taro Pharmaceuticals where Mike, now Group VP, Portfolio Management, led the global new product introduction effort. In parallel he established and led the project management system for Sun Pharma's development site in Gujarat, India, implementing a Critical Chain Project Management methodology, and building a strong PMO team.

Mike defines himself as an organizational integrator. Throughout his career he has engaged in nuanced portfolio management, new product selection, project management, and launch management, realizing billions in revenue.

As a confident strategic leader of cross-functional teams, Mike has earned a reputation for fostering collaboration among traditionally isolated units (R&D, marketing, manufacturing) to transform service levels and significantly expand market footprints.

Mike has succeeded in building productive, long-term relationships with key clients based on exceptional product knowledge, reliable service, and devotion to creating win-win outcomes.

Mike lives with his wife and family in Kfar Sava, Israel.

Also by the Author:
Spiral Staircase Project Management: A Framework to Succeed Complex-Cognitive Projects (https://www.amazon.com/dp/B06XZ78BJH)

Also by Author

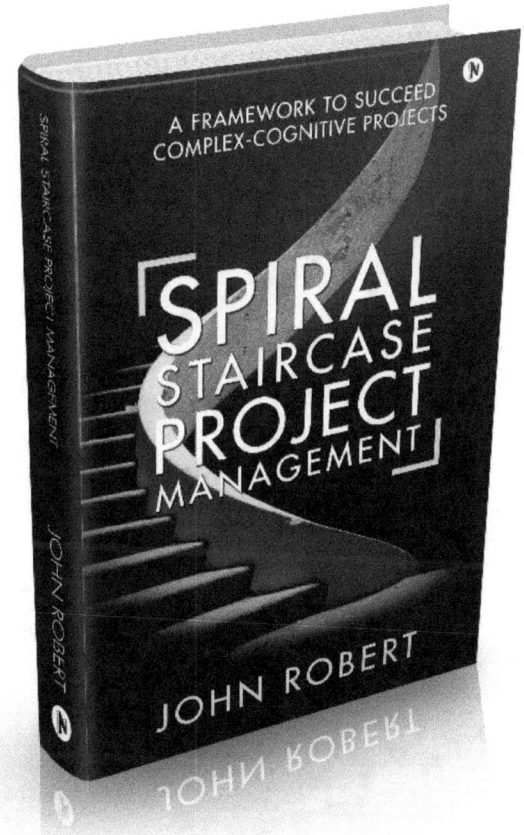

www.ingramcontent.com/pod-product-compliance
Lightning Source LLC
Chambersburg PA
CBHW071449220526
45472CB00003B/727